When a book has touched my heart to the extent where I have to put it down for a few days, I know it's a good one. The author affected me this way numerous times in her writing and after a while, I just let the tears flow, continuing to turn the pages until I had read it all. Eva has totally captured the essence of twinship in this wonderful book - how she lost her twin, Neva, tragically to cancer, how close they were throughout their lives, the battle her sweet beloved twin fought and lost. The fact she was so lost and did not know how she was going to be a "me" instead of a "we". She also shows us how there is hope and healing after twin loss - you live with them in your heart guiding you through life's journey until you meet again.

There are many "treats" afforded the reader in A ME WITHOUT WE. The author tells the stories of other twinless twins in their own words. She tries to give comfort to the grieving twin with advice of a counselor from questions of other twinless twins. She also gives resources twins can go to get help and offers advice on things she learned about loss from other twins who have already been on the journey.

A ME WITHOUT WE is a must read for twins who have lost their twins, family and friends. This gets a 5 Star from me!

—Dawn Barnett, twin to Daryl

A Me Without We

A Collection of Stories and Resources on Twin Life, Twin Loss, and Twinless Living

A Me Without We

A Collection of Stories and Resources on Twin Life, Twin Loss, and Twinless Living

EVA JO SOMBATHY,
TWIN TO NEVA

Co-Authored by Jamie Parker
Edited by Charla Haley Fitzwater and Jan Konya-Grabill

Paperback: 978-1-64085-653-0
Hardback: 978-1-64085-654-7
Ebook: 978-1-64085-655-4

Library of Congress Control Number: 2019938967

Dedication

This collection of stories, comfort, and guidance is dedicated to those of you who have been forever changed by the loss of a beloved twin. Whether you experienced a joyful life with your twin, only shared a brief but precious moment with them, or if you are the loved one of a twinless twin, this collection is written to help you find the beauty, peace, and comfort in knowing that you are not alone in your twinless-twin journey.

A special inspiration is shared with you through the book cover. As you will read, I experienced a breathtaking dream of my sweet twin shortly after she passed away. The dream was so vivid that I wanted to capture the image forever in my mind. This was the moment, a moment in the middle of my darkest days, where my twin helped me lift my chin and get busy living. I hope you find the same inspiration through this emotional collection. You are worth it – lift your chin and get busy living!

Acknowledgments

I would like to extend a special thanks to all of you who joined me in this collection. So many wonderful contributors inspired this collection and provided comfort and encouragement through my ongoing journey. You all graciously and willingly listened to my ideas about this book and helped shape it to what you see today.

To Jamie Parker, my perfect co-author, thank you for assisting me in skillfully organizing the pages and giving beautiful form to the publication. Your attention and precision were remarkable. You encouraged me to make the book better.

I really do believe people come into our lives for a reason and influence our journey. I am honored to have my name on this book but could not have done it without the following friends and family.

I am forever indebted to the willingness of my fellow twinless twins, Dawn Barnett, Charla Haley Fitzwater, Rod Cowan, Darla Barer, Crystal Hewell, and Anjy Lobelia Roemelt who willingly shared their stories of loss and living. Thank you for your compelling stories. Your insights and experiences are powerful and diverse and by sharing your stories you are helping those who are grieving deeply over twin loss, assisting them in weathering the storm, and finding peace and willpower.

Special thanks to Rocco Minichino for your wonderful art work. Thank you for sharing your incredibly artistic talents and for taking my dream and turning it into a beautiful drawing.

To my "bestie" Carolyn Burleson, MS, LPC, LCDC, MAC, you have made so many contributions to the field of counseling as you continuously display extraordinary integrative capacity and methodological sophistication. You compassionately improve the lives of those around you.

To my readers, I am so new to this process and I am certainly not an expert. My words written here are for you and for me. I hope they help us all heal and learn it is okay to hurt but we must keep living.

To my friends and editors Charla Haley Fitzwater and Jan Konya--Grabill. Thank you so much for dedicating your time to this project. My fellow twinless twins, I wish we had met under different circumstances. You so unselfishly carry the tears of so many people on your shoulders by the extraordinary work you do and support you offer to those who grieve just like you. I am so glad to call you friends.

I saved the last and most heartfelt thank you for my family. To my husband, Tim, who continues to patiently and warmly love and support me in the most difficult time of my life. He thoughtfully listened to my wild idea of writing this book and is always ready to listen as I get carried away with intensity.

My deepest appreciation to my children, Noah, Timothy, Jamie, and Jessica. Noah pulled me out of the darkest days of my life without even knowing it. He has a kind and gentle spirit which lives in a grizzly bear's body. Timothy provides endless hugs and I can't imagine getting through a day without them. My daughter, Jamie, stands a whopping 4'11" yet acts as momma bear when she sees her momma in pain and would happily follow me to the moon and back. And finally, my daughter, Jessica, who is more like me than anyone. Her independence and her confidence shine like the sun. I have a feeling she'll be the one stuck taking care of me in my old age. Each of them has a love for family and understanding that make living in grief bearable.

Table of Contents

Part III: Comfort & Resources

PART I

My Story

Things I've Learned from Being a Twin

* Toddler twins are louder than two hundred adults in a crowded restaurant.

* Twin babble could and should be an official language.

* Ketchup most certainly replaces a vibrant red hair dye for the aspiring hairdresser and her supportive twin sister.

* Two-year-old twins streaking in the back of a station wagon is quite the entertainment for small-town onlookers, and could have set the stage for mischievous adolescent years.

* Make-believe surgical procedures and limbless dolls are likely to occur when one twin loves baby dolls and the other wants to be a doctor.

* Six-year old twins can start a fire with a flint rock, especially when their father says it's only possible in the movies.

* The average response time for the fire department, when "twins started a fire by flint rock" in the backyard, is about twenty minutes . . . and, by that time, the fire is better than those in the movies.

* Twins share everything . . . I mean EVERYTHING. If not, the other will find out.

* Being super weird is always acceptable to your twin, even when you're an adult.

* Being invited to a party without your twin is torture and only happens once.

  There is always enough love.

* Standing up for one another is a given.

* Tickle-torturing younger siblings almost always involves both twins hog-tying the younger siblings together.

* There is always a look-out when twins want to be naughty.

* There is also always, always an alibi to cover your story.

* Just because one twin is great at sports, doesn't mean the other is . . . but they do get to see how awesome they'd look if they were.

* Switching places and not getting caught is priceless.

* All boys want to date twin sisters and the answer is always "no."

* Twins always have someone to tell them when that outfit makes them look fat.

* Twins hold each other's deepest secrets for eternity.

* Twins are half of a whole and carry the other with them every single day, regardless of whether they realize it or not.

Double the trouble. Double the fun.
Double the love.

The College Street Streakers

O ur story begins at conception, when one egg split into two, causing us to separate for the very first time. We were connected - both physically and emotionally - meant to physically mirror one another yet hold unique and complementary characteristics, while emotionally bound together tighter than the last hug we ever shared. Identical twins born August 14th, 1968, we were labeled "Twin A" and "Twin B." We left the hospital with our perfectly placed bracelets, which were kept there for weeks to help family and friends identify us. My mother used to tell us there were very few ways to tell us apart. We were told that Neva had a rounder face as an infant and during childhood, but we never agreed.

Over the years, the two of us spent countless hours shuffling through dozens of photographs which always revealed two identical, chubby-faced babies. Mom would claim that she "just knew who her babies were," and she likely corrected hundreds of people about who was Eva and who was Neva. I think most parents have that special bond with their children; they can sense their different energies, blindly know their presence and touch, and share magical emotions with a simple glance. Nevertheless, my twin and I forever joked, and sometimes really believed, that we were switched at birth and maybe more than once. I would usually end the joke with a little shove and deny any chance of her having the better name. I am Eva Jo and her name is Neva Joyce.

It is beyond the most challenging endeavor to explain the connection between twins. Regardless of their age, the bond between them just can't be described. Most people cannot comprehend and will never have an opportunity to feel the remarkable experience of sharing life with a twin sibling. Can you imagine sharing every moment in life with someone else, the same someone else? Experiencing your first touch, first love, first fight, first adventure, first secret, first heartache, learning to walk, talk, play, work, and share together. All stages of life, from conception to adulthood, each twin has shared with their one special person, their twin. Studies suggest emotion starts in the womb, which may explain why babies in utero jump when they hear loud noises. Were they frightened? Pleasure could be expressed as thumb sucking and anxiety as an increase in heart rate. Could the feeling of love and a profound emotional connection develop at this stage of life as well?

As any mother of multiple small children would agree about their own, my mother claimed that we were quite the entertainers as babies, a modern Lucy and Ethel if you will. She was convinced we developed our own language and we would babble to each other, clearly understanding what the other was saying. Family members claimed they never needed a television when we were around, and we were proud of this honorable mention. My aunt would make our hysterical stories the talk of the town, especially the one where we became known as the College Street Streakers.

As toddlers, we loved to ride around in our Aunt Mildred's station wagon. This was long before seatbelt laws were enforced, so we thought we had license to roam. With the hot Texas sun beating down into the car, Aunt Mildred would take off her cardigan and slightly crack the back window for airflow. Who didn't love those big rear windows back then? I know we sure did — and we were hot, too! So, we nonchalantly decided to crawl toward the fresh air and take off our clothes! Neva and I argued throughout adulthood about who threw the first diaper at the poor woman driving behind us. All we knew is that both bare-bottomed babies were spotted by onlookers who were dodging the flying diapers being thrown out the back. The College Street Streakers — our first nickname.

Another story that was often told involved Neva and me as cupids. Neva and I are two of four girls, right in the middle of an older sister and a younger sister. Needless to say, our single mother had a difficult time finding love after our older sister and we were born. Three small, rambunctious girls — ouch! We were told, however, that our mother's luck changed, all thanks to Neva and me, when we were only two years old. We were playing in the front yard at our Aunt Mildred's house when a young man approached the walkway to speak to our mother. He worked for the city removing trees and was taking a short break from the summer heat. He noticed how cute the two of us were and with our mother's nod of approval, we quickly jumped in his lap. The man and our mother quickly fell in love and were married shortly after the introduction. I suppose you could thank Neva and me for being our mother's cupid.

As we entered elementary school, it was nearly impossible to tell us apart physically. But, Neva was the smart one and I was the talker. Among our friends, we had been known to swap places many times throughout our childhood, but I must admit the best switcheroo happened in second grade. We swapped places every day in school for nearly four weeks! Only a few friends knew and they made it difficult to keep from giggling throughout the day. We finally got caught when my grades started miraculously improving while Neva's rolled down hill quickly. The cherry-on-top of our mischief was Neva's first, and only, report card revealing she "talks too much." We both giggled conspiratorially and agreed that the punishment was well worth the fun we had impersonating each other. I'll bet the teachers got a kick out of it also – wouldn't you?

We were both very active and played sports most of our childhood, but Neva was definitely the athlete. Although she begged me to participate in sports with her, I would much rather have been a dancer. I had always dreamed of ballet, dance, and gymnastics, though I chose my sister's side in sports instead. It was odd that even though we shared such identical physical characteristics, we still had very unique personalities. It amazes me how two people can be so connected yet so different at the same time. I always enjoyed participating in Neva's outdoor adventures like fort building or go-kart construction, but you'd better believe my baby dolls tagged along and helped, too. Now that I think about it, I can honestly say that Neva never participated in playing house, dressing up Barbies, or making supper for my lovely "pretend children." She was just not that kind of girl. Thankfully, I had my younger sister who indulged in those activities with me. Our eldest sister played the role of teacher or supervisor; back then we just called her 'bossy.' "Don't do that, Eva!" "That's not how you do it, Neva!" She was certainly our little momma when our mother couldn't be around. Neva and I loved and cherished the special moments with our sisters, but those relationships were nowhere close to the electromagnetic connection between the two of us.

Some identical twins become slightly less identical as they grow into adulthood, but as pre-teens, we continued to identically resemble each other, although we had started to branch out in our choices of clothing to reflect our individual preferences. Most people were interested and humored by our identical mannerisms, yet individual styles. To tell us apart or describe who we were, strangers and even friends would try to define us. The fat one, the pretty one, the smart one, the boyish one. Yet, as unflattering and sometimes cruel as some of the descriptions were, we never wished to look like anyone else except each other. We never had that typical sibling rivalry nor did we ever compete with one another for attention or love from others. The only fights we ever had were pretend wrestling and that was mostly due to prime-time television, where we would mimic the moves of famous wrestlers. As you can probably conclude at this point, Neva was the stronger one and took it easy on me. Every now and then I would get in a good hit or move that would push her buttons and I knew to take off running. As a mother of four now, I know fighting between siblings is normal. My two girls argued until their faces were blue when they were younger; similar to my boys, who fought into adulthood. However, I think the reason Neva and I didn't fight was because we truly needed each other.

To say our home life was unstable would be a drastic understatement. Our biological father never claimed us as his own, so our older sister had "her dad" from that relationship. Our younger sister also had "her dad" from our mother's later marriage (thanks to us, remember!) He was our step-father, brought together by mine and Neva's cupid-like actions when we were two. Although I now have immense respect for him and love him dearly, he had a rough childhood and did not know how to show love, only stress and anger when we were kids. He cared for my mother and three babies under the age of three the only way he knew how. My mother and step-father later had our little sister, making a house of five females and one male. That certainly doesn't justify his abuse, however. He was tough and mean at times, and when we thought the fights and aggression were bad, they only got worse. Christmases came and passed with broken and damaged presents, we were locked outside with only water in the middle of terrible Texas summers, and his yell down the hall made the tiny hairs on our necks stand straight up. These were some of the many times in our lives that we knew we needed each other. We would huddle together in our room and hold each other until the storms would calm.

Neva and I were all we ever had growing up. On the outside we may have been a beautiful family, but on the inside, Neva and I were caught in the middle of what became a loveless, abusive marriage, where we were the punching bags. I'm certain our parents and family members questioned why we slept together through high school, literally all the way through our senior year! I had my own bed but it was cold, unsafe, and frightening. Together we felt safe whether we were or not. Eighteen years of nightly sleepovers, talking, giggling, and crying. How we ever slept I will never know, but we knew every single detail about each other. Nothing was off limits. We even exchanged the occasional reality check if one of us needed advice or words of encouragement. We never held back or sugar-coated anything. Can you imagine going through every day of life knowing there is someone who loves you unconditionally? She is your teacher, student, critic, and biggest fan. We shared countless laughs and accomplishments and encouraged each other to be the best we could. We shared, celebrated, and learned from each other's successes and failures. There was never a moment where we couldn't rely on one another. We were best friends.

As we entered adulthood, we wanted to explore separate interests and form our own identities. Sadly, we drifted apart a little during this time. It was difficult establishing who we were as individuals when we had always had the other on our side. We broadened our circle of friends and started dating, as most young adults do. I decided to leave home as quickly as possible and got married at a young age. It deeply saddened me to hear later in life that she resented the fact I left her. She once told me that I left her in "that home" by herself and it hurt her. She was right. She had no one. Those years I will never get back, and I regret not being there when she really needed me.

However, a new baby brings everyone back together, right? When I had my first child she might as well been Neva's instead of mine. Neva loved my daughter and took her everywhere. So much for not playing with baby dolls when we were young! She waited for the real-life baby. I would have never thought she would love a child as much as she loved my daughter. Our voices were so similar, my daughter would just stare at Neva with a look of confusion but smile and laugh at the familiarity. It's funny because we ended up sharing this experience with all our children. Even our grandchildren would laugh and make comments about how we sounded so much alike.

Shortly after my first daughter was born, Neva joined the Army in hopes of discovering herself as a young woman. Honestly, I never once worried about her during this endeavor. I knew that her strong and loving personality would find great friends, and I knew in my heart that she would return home safely. Selfishly, I suppose, I worried more about myself. I remember feeling lonely without her nearby, even with a growing family and new marriage to keep me busy. While she was stationed in different countries, I felt as if the stars in my sky weren't even connected to the same sky she gazed upon. Yet, although feeling and knowing that we were so far apart, I would experience intense senses of empathy, strong enough to generate physical sensations. I felt pain as if it were her pain. During these times, I would question the emotional and physical pain I experienced. . . where was this coming from? Was I ill or injured, or did I regret letting her leave? Other times, I felt happiness and pride, as if I were the one honoring our great country. I would talk to her, dream about her, reference her in conversations, and I was convinced that I subconsciously knew exactly how she felt and thought about everything. At one point, I remember thinking I was psychotic, laughing at myself and my "imaginary friend" I had created. Sporadic emotions constantly surfaced, and I could sense the danger, fear, love, and happiness that my sister was feeling.

When Neva returned home, I told her about these crazy, yet robust experiences I had. I was slightly embarrassed but knew I must express the odd sensations I had, feeling as if I knew exactly what she was going through. As I spoke sheepishly, her face shifted into a look of disbelief and amazement; a look not unlike a child's face when seeing a magician pull a rabbit from his hat. We had known our entire lives that we shared a connection – that with only one look we knew what the other was thinking. However, how could this be real? We were thousands of miles apart and didn't speak often. It was as if our eyes, hearts, and souls laughed at the ignorance of our brains for not knowing the connection we shared. At that moment, we knew wholeheartedly that we were feeling each other's emotions, and it was at this point we both realized how powerful and how real the connection between twins is.

Society and researchers alike have studied this idea many times throughout history. The myths, horror stories, mysteries, and crystal-ball coincidences of "twin telepathy," where it is believed, and sometimes not believed, that twins share emotions, pain, and connections that no other two human beings can experience. Some research suggests that although it is more typical in identical twins, like Neva and me, fraternal twins can also experience this beautiful and scary phenomenon. We were certainly living proof! Being thousands of miles and several countries apart, we felt it, experienced it, and lived it.

When Neva's military career ended, she ventured to Idaho to start her family while I remained in Texas with mine. We had numerous experiences where we "just had a feeling and decided to call" the other. We actually called each other at the exact same time on one occasion. I had an overwhelming sense she needed me and developed an instant uncomfortable, butterfly-type feeling in my stomach. I could hear her calling my name and I knew she was in some sort of distress. At the exact moment I picked up the phone to call her, she called me because she was in labor with her first baby. As our lives grew and went on, we found there were times we didn't talk as much as we could have. We lived in different places most of the time and grew into our own routines. There were times we went months without talking or seeing each other, but when we were together, all we needed was to look at the other to know what the other was thinking and feeling. I loved that the most about us. For a few years we lived in the same city and had a beautiful family life together. Dinners on Sundays, evening walks, family movies, and sharing the joys and hardships of life. Whether we were near, far, speaking or not, Neva was very much a part of me. She made me whole. Now, without her here, I find her in the mirror.

The Devastating News

Thanksgiving used to be my favorite holiday. I loved to host the gathering of friends and family over a beautiful feast, watching my grandchildren play together, cheering on our Dallas Cowboys in the afternoon, and Black Friday shopping at the wee hours of the following morning with my two daughters. Thanksgiving 2016 forever changed my love for this holiday. Neva and I would visit one another every few years on either Thanksgiving or Christmas, and in 2016 we had planned to celebrate Christmas together, only one month away. While my daughters and I had just finished our long stretch of adrenaline-boosting shopping, my phone rang and I saw her name. I thought, "A phone call at 9 a.m. on the Friday following Thanksgiving?" I had just talked to her not even 24 hours ago. My heart sank immediately, and I could feel this was not a good call.

Neva was a very busy and successful business woman. Most of our phone calls were at night, after our busy days had calmed down. Even on the holidays she was busy. We had briefly chatted on Thanksgiving Day. She laughed, and I rolled my eyes at the fact that she was hard at work as usual. She began telling me, apologetically, that she hadn't been feeling well, and that she didn't want to concern me, which is why she didn't mention it before. That morning, however, Neva received alarming results from medical tests that were performed earlier in the week. There was no diagnosis at that point but she was scared. So was I. She continued to explain the tests, her doctor's concerns, and the next steps. It was only noise to me then . . . background rambling as my soul froze and memories of our lives flashed in the forefront of my thoughts. The pain and innocent worry in her voice instantly struck my heart like a dagger. Neither of us ever had to ask for support from the other. We just knew when it was needed. And I knew she needed me then – to be there with her. I was packed and in the car within the hour to make the 17-hour trip from Texas to Ohio.

I had made the long drive countless times before. I lived in Ohio for a few years, while most of my family and friends lived in Texas. I frequently made the trip to visit and, honestly, it had never bothered me. The drive gave me the much-needed break from my daily routine, time to think and self-reflect, precious "me time" alone in a car.

This time it was different. The trip seemed to last for days, and each highway and gas station appeared to be the same. Was I driving in circles? Would I ever get there? Or was this house of mirrors only here to haunt me from what was about to change my life forever? When I arrived, Neva and I hugged, and I could sense the fear in her body. Fear that I had never felt from her before. Fear that I suspect she had also felt in me because we both simultaneously squeezed tighter. She was the strong one between the two of us; she never showed that kind of emotion.

We walked into the living room and she began to tell me what she had been hiding for the past few weeks. Her doctor suggested a procedure to examine the digestive problems she had been experiencing. They originally thought it was her gall bladder, which would make sense considering gall bladder issues have troubled many of our family members in the past. The surgery, however, resulted in the discovery of large masses inside her stomach, nothing close to a gall bladder issue. We impatiently waited by the phone for days until it finally rang . . . tears instantly filled her eyes as the voice on the other end of the line stated the possibility of cancer. I've seen similar stories in movies and have heard stories from friends and co-workers, but never did I ever think I would be sitting here listening to my twin sister receive news that she might have cancer. And not just cancer, but large cancerous masses in her stomach. What did that even mean? Anxiety and anger instantly enraged my soul. I wanted it fixed right then! No, we cannot wait a week for additional testing – this is my sister!

I quickly flew home to Texas to get personal and family matters aligned before making my way back to Ohio that same week. Neva had an exploratory surgery where doctors examined the affected areas and took samples to determine the diagnosis. And there we were again, nine days later, ironically waiting for news that we did not want to hear in the first place. This was certainly not like the time Neva and I snuck out of the house as teenagers, then frightfully waited under the covers because we thought our parents heard the window shut. Nor was it like the time we decided to cut our younger sister's hair and awaited punishment from our mother because it was not as symmetrical as she thought it should be. Nope, this time was different. We awaited the fate of . . . us.

While we sat there holding hands, like we had many times before, Neva was diagnosed with Adenoma-Peritoneal Cancer.

Game Faces

As the pain, sorrow, and fear turned into hate for the disease, Neva and I made a plan, a pact if you will, to fight back. I found myself gearing up for battle aside my adventurous and competitive sister who was never defeated. "F- you, Cancer, you can't have her!" I found myself constantly repeating these words to remind my heart that we were fighting back and not to give up. I vowed to be with her every step of the way and as much as I physically could. Her wife, Brenda, had been in my life for more than 20 years, and I wanted to be there for her also. Brenda is a beautiful soul who, together with Neva, stood in a world that didn't always accept who they were. Their personal life was always kept private and their friendship far exceeded the average relationship of a married couple. So, there we were, the three of us, starring at the face of this terrible sickness.

Every two weeks was my plan. I would return to Neva's side every two weeks and stay for as long as I could. Brenda would keep me posted every day I wasn't there, and I would give her relief while I was there. I was wholeheartedly devoted to this routine for as long as Neva and Brenda needed me and until my Neva was healthy again. We quickly discovered, though, that no matter how much we planned and pep-talked each other, the outcome we desired the most might not be our fate in the very near future.

Neva started chemotherapy in mid-January, less than two months after we got the initial news. Over those prior months, however, her health had drastically worsened. She lost twenty to thirty pounds in a matter of weeks and lethargy seized the energetic sister I had always known. The first round of treatment severely aggravated the masses and the cancer began to grow at an exponential rate. Brenda and I decided it was time to call our family back home and Neva's children, who were in Idaho. They had known about the cancer and they spoke to Neva daily, but this call was one that no young adult is prepared to hear about their mother. My pain-stricken heart didn't want to give the news, but I knew they needed to see her before her health and appearance had declined too much.

The last time I drove from Texas to Ohio to see Neva was also the time I brought our dad with me. He and Neva had not spoken in many years, and I was unsure how she would react to him being there. She was more reserved than I was with her forgiveness toward our dad. They had a strong bond when we were children; she was sort of like the son he never had. But as we grew up, she realized that his temper was out-of-control and she couldn't forgive him. She did, however, ask about him often and would reminisce about the good times they shared. She told me once that she wished she could let go of those bad memories and talk to him again. I think they both shared a similar pride that was not easily broken. When we got to the hospital, Neva was asleep from another exploratory surgery performed earlier that morning. Dad was nervous to see her but told me he wanted to hold her hand, apologize, and tell her he loves her one last time. As I walked into the room, Neva woke up and immediately knew something was up. She

yelled, "What did you do, butthead? I can see it on your face."
I smirked awkwardly and let her know that Daddy was here,
in the hall. She stared at me a moment, as if she were trying
to put the words in order, to make sure she understood what
I was saying. She just replied, "Okay," in an oddly accepting
manner.

I will never forget what happened next for the rest of my
life. The moment Neva eagerly and impatiently gazed around
that hospital curtain and saw her daddy walking in, all the
anger and resentment they carried over the years instantly disappeared. It blew out the window like a refreshing gust of wind
on a hot summer day. They both cried and held each other,
speechless. The past was no longer important. That moment;
that was important. Daddy and Neva shared stories with the
family over the following few days. Stories about fixing up
old Volkswagens and their favorite family dog. They laughed
about the good times they had together, and they cried about
the present, forgiving each other for their mistakes.

Neva's wife, children, grandchildren, father, sisters, niece,
and nephew were all by her side in late January when doctors
gave the news. The cancer was too aggressive and was multi-
plying by the day. They sadly exclaimed that we should enjoy
the weeks we possibly had left. As we all tried to compose
our teary eyes while inundating the doctors for answers, Neva
looked over at me and said, "I just don't feel like I'm dying."
My heart was broken and my head in disbelief. I kept a journal
of my final few days with Neva and my entry from this day
is still difficult for me to read:

What it's like to be a twin? I have been asked this a lot in
my life. The best way I can describe it is this: I have the most
beautiful family tree. Four amazing children, an incredible
husband, and five of the most beautiful (and spoiled) grandchildren in the world. Anyone who knows me would say I am
with them always and would literally give my life for them.
Yet . . . by powers outside of my control, they consume only

half of my heart. The other half belongs to Neva. We are all we have ever had. I am not sure what this monster "cancer" has in store for us but I know, deep down, that my heart will never be the same.

On February 3, Neva was released from the hospital to hospice care. I sobbed as I called family and friends, telling them I wished I could give them good news, praying that this whole thing was just one big nightmare, and hoping that we could all wake up and she'd be healed. I explained that the reality, though, was Neva left the hospital to go into hospice. There was nothing more doctors could do. At the rate the cancer had grown in such a short period of time, the best thing at that point was for Neva to be comfortable. I asked everyone to pray for Brenda and Neva's kids. And to pray that she wouldn't suffer any longer.

I continued to travel back and forth as I had promised. I mastered the trip and was there in fourteen hours instead of seventeen. During one of my visits, Neva was feeling great and explained to me and hospice that she just wasn't ready to die. She wanted alternative treatment and not just the comfort medication she had been receiving. Of course, hospice couldn't help with that, so we decided to look elsewhere for care. Feeling hopeful, Brenda and I diligently searched for a Cancer treatment center nearby. Neva was eager to fight for as long as she could, which motivated us to fight also. We found a facility in Columbus, Ohio and they accepted Neva as a patient right away. We had the best possible team looking at her and Brenda and I felt relieved and hopeful. We saw a medical oncologist, surgical oncologist, wound care specialist, nutritionist, infection control specialist, and three primary doctors within the first 24 hours. At one point, I remember counting a total of eleven doctors, researchers, and professionals discussing her rare disease outside her door. They were determined to find a solution for her . . . for us.

There wasn't a dry eye in the room when the team regretfully gave us the news. Neva was just too sick for treatment. The expanding cancer prevented her from eating and her health declined from there. Developing infections around her feeding port, together with the inability to consume food or water by mouth, there was not much hope for her health to improve enough for cancer treatment. And, as we all knew, without the chemotherapy treatment she couldn't fight the cancer. At that point, Neva decided to go back home and search for unconventional methods to slow the cancer, anything that would buy precious time. While driving the one-hour ride back to her home on February 13th, Neva asked that I submit the following message on her social media page:

"Wanted to send a quick update. Thank you to all who have kept a strong vigilance in praying and spending countless time trying to find a solution. Eva and Brenda, thanks for today :-) we aren't done yet, I love you."

Neva was a fighter. She never took "no" for an answer. When someone gave her an excuse or told her it wasn't possible, she returned a look that sent chills down their spine. I would always laugh when I saw the look – it meant business. I never realized I would miss that look . . . until now. When we returned to her home that February evening, I knew she felt defeated. She didn't have a game plan or want to talk about how the doctors must be wrong. She felt that the end was near, and there was nothing she could do but be strong for us.

Neva wanted to be at home. She spent a couple of weeks trying unconventional methods for pain and anxiety. Marijuana and protein suppositories raised her spirits and energy, so we enjoyed the precious time making memories. It was like we were teenagers again. We made plaster cast molds holding hands, took too many (but not enough) selfies, stayed up late watching movies, and video chatted with old friends.

She even wrote me a note and put in the hand mold just in case it ever broke.

In the past, when Neva and I would visit one another, she would get in a mood and want to cuddle. I would give her a sarcastic look and tell her we are grown women – we are not cuddling. During those final days together, though, cuddling was all I wanted. I wanted to lie in her bed and hold her. I wanted to touch her skin, her face, her hands. I knew I would never be able to do that again. I found myself recording our conversations, even recording the silence as we sat; anything I could do to remember and hear her forever.

During those precious weeks at Neva's home, her health quickly faded. Brenda, her children, and I knew we couldn't care for her during this time. The pain only strengthened and it could no longer be controlled at home. As we drove Neva back to the hospice facility, we prayed together, cried together, and sat in silent disbelief together. We knew we were driving to the end. The end of this journey with our precious Neva. Our solider. Our rock. My beloved twin.

My "Ides of March"

It was now the beginning of March, my least favorite month of all. The month that gives me anxiety and turns me into an overprotective mother and wife. For those Shakespeareans out there, you may appreciate my reference. For others who have been affected by loss or multiple losses around the same time-frame, you may appreciate or empathize with my superstition.

Shakespeare's words, "Beware the Ides of March," will forever conjure up a dark and gloomy connotation (sensation? emotion? impression? perception?) that tends to make people uncomfortable around mid-March. As Roman history reveals to us, the "Ides" was how ancient Rome identified the first full moon of a given month. During this ancient time, the Ides was typically between the 13th and 15th day of every month. Since the Ides of March once signified the new year, ancient Romans typically celebrated and rejoiced on this day, by what I envision probably involved too much wine and some form of a flashy ball descending down a wooden flag pole. Shakespeare's Julius Caesar, however, changed this day for Rome.

The Ides of March will live in infamy as the day Julius Caesar was betrayed and brutally murdered, and for centuries beyond his death, modern society will continue to associate death, sorrow, and gloom with this day, now generally recognized on March 15. Invasions, severe weather, ozone degradation, global health scares, and not to mention the cancellation of the "Ed Sullivan Show" in 1971 - these were just a few worldwide bad omens that occurred on that day. Being a spiritual and superstitious woman, I believe my family carries our own "Ides of March" omens. Yet, ours seems to last the entire month.

Every family member I can remember from my childhood through adulthood has died in March. No kidding. My sisters and I did research on our family tree years ago and found this to be hair-raisingly true. From our infant cousin to aunts, uncles, and great-great grandparents, our family seems to be cursed with deaths in March. We may have not known all these relatives, but as we grew older we became more superstitious of the cursed month.

One of Neva's and my favorite people on earth, our Uncle Roe, died suddenly in March of 1999. Uncle Roe was our protector when we were children. He was our safe place to run. His arms were always open, and he was the best tire-swing pusher in North Texas. When we were growing up, Aunt Mildred and Uncle Roe lived on the same street. We were at their house daily making mud pies, pretending, playing with the neighboring children, and hiding behind Uncle Roe's shadow when our parents were fighting or upset with us. His death was my first real experience with the tragic March omen. However, knowing what I knew about our misfortune, I knew it wouldn't be my last.

March also marked a devastating tragedy for our mother when she was a child. She experienced something that, thankfully, most of us have never and will never experience, something that shaped who she was as a child and who she became as an adult. In March 1958, our mother was a young and energetic girl nearing her tenth birthday. She had a large family that included her mother, father, and three brothers. Being the only girl and one of the youngest, our mom enjoyed being her father's princess and playing with her rambunctious brothers. Her family enjoyed outdoor activities, so it was no surprise to find them at the lake on the weekends.

On March 11, 1958, after a day filled with boating at a local Texas lake, my grandfather was driving his family home down a rural two-lane highway. The reason was never released and maybe not even known, but my grandfather mistakenly swerved into oncoming traffic causing a fatal impact.

My mother, a 9-year-old girl with no seatbelt, was the sole survivor. At that instant, an innocent child lost her mother, father, all her siblings, and the childhood she had known. Although I was not fortunate enough to know my grandparents or uncles, my heart breaks every time I read that newspaper article and think of that day. As any other parent, spouse, sibling, or decent human being can relate, I cannot fathom the pain, heartbreak, and loss that comes with that magnitude of trauma.

March 2017 was certainly no exception to our misfortune. When we received Neva's news the past November, my family was also managing devastating news about my mother. My mother had been on kidney dialysis for more than two years. She began to lose her eye sight and developed early-onset dementia during the second year of treatment. My sisters and I knew she couldn't care for herself, so we moved her into an assisted living facility where she was constantly sur- rounded by me and my siblings, her grandchildren, and her great-grandchildren.

At the beginning of 2017, her health had progressively worsened. Dialysis and diabetes had taken a toll on her organs and while I was traveling back and forth to see Neva, doctors started talking to the family about required surgeries and the possibility of amputations for my mother to continue living. My mother had always told us that she never wanted to be at a point where she was unaware of who she was. Since being diagnosed with diabetes, she also knew the horror stories of amputations and that was her biggest fear.

My mother lived her life to the fullest and wanted to be surrounded by her grandchildren always; her destiny in life was to love us. She wanted to love her grandbabies and be with them for as long as she could. She never missed a soccer game and was always available to watch the children when asked. She certainly didn't want her family to see her helpless and unaware of who they or she was.

March 3 was the day that introduced my "Ides of March" for the year. We had known that my mother was resisting the doctors' recommendations and that she was examining her options. As children, you hope you never have to make decisions about whether your parents should live or die. My mother proved to be stronger than we had ever seen her when she made her own decision that day. While I was driving through Memphis, Tennessee, my mother decided that she would have no more surgeries and no more dialysis. She was sincere and content with her decision and she fully understood what the decision meant for her life.

We were told that in her condition she wouldn't live longer than five days without dialysis. Besides being very ill, bedridden, and facing amputations, she selfishly admitted that she couldn't bear to experience one of her children passing before she did. My mother experienced so much pain from losing loved ones in her life. How could we force her to continue fighting for us after all that she had been through with losing her family?

During the nine days following her decision, family swarmed in and out of my mother's room. They showered her with love and comfort, reminiscing on stories of the good ole' days, listening to her favorite Elvis songs, and sharing video calls with Neva in Ohio. My mother gave her last hug and kiss to her grandchildren on March 11 and passed away on March 12, 2017.

Hollow Seashell
of a Heart

I am very fortunate and appreciative of the time I was able to spend with my mother during her final days. With my frequent travels to be with Neva, and knowing I wanted to be with her through the end, I made the decision to spend time with my mom but knew I couldn't stay by her side. As I was visiting with my mom on March 9, knowing it could very well be the last time I hugged her neck, Brenda called to confirm that Neva had taken a turn for the worse. Unfit to make the trip alone, my husband and youngest son instantly drove me to Ohio for the final time. I sat in the backseat weeping and praying for Neva to hold on until I got there. We arrived to find her unresponsive; she was leaving us. She was leaving me.

As we neared the day that I knew was inevitable and too close, Neva began to fade and in and out of consciousness. The Neva who I knew everything about, the one who could feel my presence and I hers, the Neva who was strong, courageous, and never defeated, my Neva, had left her body that lay there next me. Although her heart was still beating gently, I knew she was no longer in there. I held her hand, told her I loved her and subconsciously knew she was responding from somewhere else. Before this time, Neva read the bible daily. She had strong faith and knew where she was going. As I sat there holding her hand, sobbing, I reassured her and myself that there was a higher power and greater purpose behind my fear, sadness, and anger.

Knowing that her soul would soon pass, I prepared myself to call the funeral home to start the arrangements for Brenda. Talk about an out of body experience! The words came out of my mouth as if I were in a slow-motion scene of a movie. The room suddenly blurred and reality hit me like a boulder falling from the side of a Colorado highway. Did I just say my sister to the woman on the other end of the phone? "WAKE UP, EVA, THIS IS A TERRIBLE NIGHTMARE!" I said to myself.

After a moment of silence during my attempt to internally wake myself from this horrifying nightmare, the woman at the funeral home gently spoke, asking me to take a deep breath. She sympathetically talked me through the process and kindly said she would have to ask me some questions. The hollow black tunnel of disbelief sharpened, and I knew I couldn't continue the conversation as she asked the most basic question that was to be expected. "Ma'am, do you know Miss Neva's birthdate?"

Of course, I knew her birthday! It was our birthday! The same birthday we shared for forty-eight years! The day that carried memories of joint wishes and shared songs, with not a single year passing where it was only Neva's day or only my day . . . a day that we planned to share until we were a hundred years old, or at least closer to it. I became so inconsolable that I cannot remember if I hung up the phone or stopped talking until the woman hung up on me. I was paralyzed by the realization that our once-special day together would never be the same again. It kept playing repeatedly in my head. Selfishness found its way into my heart. How could I ever face that day again? What will our birthday be like without my other half? How can there be a me, without the fullness of we?

The Friday before Neva passed, as I lay next to her reading, a sudden presence engulfed the room. I instantly knew someone was in there with us and I was terrified to look up from my book to check on Neva or to look around. Although I know it is commonly mocked and disbelieved, I am not ashamed to admit that I have had the gift of clairvoyance for as long as I can remember. This time was different, though. I could feel the presence stronger than any time before and could pinpoint the specific corner of the room.

A moment later, my niece walked in the room, gave me a startled look, and quickly dashed out sobbing. As I followed her out, she exclaimed, "Someone is in that room with my mom!" Unbeknownst to me, my niece had the same sense that I did. She confirmed the exact location where she felt his presence, which was the same corner in which I had sensed the presence. We both referred to him as "He." We didn't know who he was, just that he was a man. Hours later, the room filled with spirits, and silhouettes of different sizes surrounded Neva. By that evening, the male presence was now at the foot of the bed. I sensed a tall skinny silhouette; the sensation so strong that I could now paint a picture of his outline in my mind. I knew why he was here, but who (and what) was this man?

During that night, as we all tried to get some rest, Neva had started gasping for air. It was the "death rattle" from what I understand. She had all the signs that her impending death was near. Nurses rushed in to pray as we cried in sorrow. We knew it was time to let go so Neva knew it was okay to pass. We expressed our love and appreciation for her in our lives and assured her we would be okay once she was gone. Although those words came out of my mouth, I wasn't sure if the latter would be true.

The nurses administered medication to weaken the rattling sound and increased her oxygen for comfort, but think those efforts were mainly for the family laying nearby, to comfort us, because Neva was no longer suffering. As the frightful events calmed and Neva's body continued to fight for life, I noticed the spirit, "he," was no longer there with us. I sat straight up totally confused. Where had he gone?

Moments later, a feeling of relief entered my soul. I felt Neva now . . . again. I hadn't felt her true presence in days. Her new presence was not in her body, though. Instead, she was in the room trying to comfort us while we slept. Her body may have still been functioning, but her spirit had passed. As I lay there in the dark, with my eyes wide open, Neva's presence lingered and finally came to my side. I felt her ask me to take care of Brenda and, before her presence left, I felt her hold me with assurance, confirming that she would always be with me, that I'd know it with a random smile.

I consider myself grounded and well-educated and, aside from the occasional feeling of spirits nearby, I had never encountered anything like this before. In the room that night, Neva was beautifully dressed in white. She was a wispy, flowy spirit, who was totally at peace. I had never in my life used the words wispy and flowy to describe something. But those were the words that came to me that day to describe her presence.

Neva and I shared the same faith in Christ. Sadly, however, I questioned my faith more and more over the months leading up to her death. I found myself hoping and praying that eternal life in heaven was not fictional. I didn't understand how this was it. You live with happiness and sorrow and then you just die? Neva restored my faith that evening. She helped me realize that this was not "it" . . . there is something higher and more meaningful after death. As her spirit left my presence, I sobbed myself to sleep knowing this upcoming journey would be difficult but she would be by my side.

I woke up the next morning shaking from the events that occurred overnight. I knew in my heart that the man in the room the day before was there to take Neva to heaven. Neva always believed she had a guardian angel and that it was our grandfather we never met, Marvin Lewis. She grew up being compared to Marvin and we were even named after his wife and our grandmother, LaNeva. I have seen pictures of Marvin and know a lot about him through my research of my mother's childhood accident. I truly believe the man that day and night was him. What did it all mean, though? Was Marvin's spirit actually there? Does God send angels in a recognizable physical form to offer comfort for us as we enter the next journey? Is she really . . . gone?

My niece, who had the same experience as I did, awoke crying and exclaimed that she knew her mother's soul was no longer there. We both knew it. Although hesitant to do so, I shared the experience with Brenda. I knew I could no longer be there as Neva's soul, her spirit, had left. Brenda sobbed as I told her about Marvin and Neva's presence around us.

As I left Ohio to travel home, my heart felt like a hollow seashell washed up on the shore, helpless and wishing to be unbroken and full again. I literally didn't feel one thing. I could tell my husband was concerned as I gazed emotionless out the window. My mother had passed on March 12th. I wasn't there to hold her hand or protect my children as they saw their grandmother die. Then, one day later, on March 13th, my sister, my twin, and half of me died, too.

The realization hit me when I got home to Texas. I will never forget that feeling of complete heartbreak and hopelessness. I dropped to the ground in my front yard while every horrendous emotion ripped through me: devastation, heartbreak, sadness, and anger. The impact was unbelievable. My heart, breath, and soul were stripped from my body and I thought I was going to die. My darling, beautiful, Neva was gone; I just wanted to hold her one more time.

Every part of me was heavy with grief and sorrow for many months after Neva died. I felt as if I could pass out at any moment. I got to the point where I couldn't speak, and I don't even remember if I cried. This nasty dark cave was a place of deep sorrow and depression. I still have days when I walk by her picture or the beautiful hand mold and think to myself, "Is this for real? Did that really happen?"

Life Without Her

As many of you can relate, my life has vastly changed since Neva left my side. There isn't an hour that passes when I haven't thought of her and longed to see her face. I have days of grief-stricken sadness, where I find myself in bed paralyzed in disbelief. I tell myself it's a normal part of loss and I'm learning to cope and talk myself "off the ledge." I have found that time really does help with the pain and, although I know the pain will never go away, I now have hope and fond memories to help me carry on.

I found this poem that reminds me I am not alone. I would like to share it with you because it helped me understand the emotions that I was unable to describe to myself and others around me.

To lose a spouse is a tragedy, to lose a child perhaps the greatest tragedy most of us could imagine; but everyone had an identity before becoming a spouse or a parent. A twin is never anything but a twin until separation by death, and there is no way of untwinning except by death. In the most intimate of bereavements, the surviving twin finds the foundation of his or her own identity undermined because twinhood bestows the singular oddity of a plural identity.

- Rosemary Stark, Twin to Sheila

I still cannot comprehend or relate to a singular identity. I have always been part of two. Will I ever feel whole again? Will I ever discover or identify myself as singular?

I often look in the mirror searching for her and seeking her guidance. I occasionally feel her presence and smile, just like she said I would. However, I don't feel like me anymore and I sometimes question who I am. Loneliness is common and sometimes too overwhelming and unbearable.

We were supposed to grow old together somewhere on a beach. We imagined that it would just be the two of us once our spouses had passed away. We joked about that scenario since it seemed like the women in our family always lived to an old age. How is it possible that she will forever be 48? Each year I will age without her physically by my side. I still have a hard time wrapping my mind around that.

Six months after she died I fell into a very deep and dark depression. I did not want to exist in this world any longer. I felt like my love for my children, grandchildren, and husband could not get me out of this one. Friends kept saying, "Eva, you have to take care of yourself." I never understood why people said that to those who lose a loved one. I had no idea what it meant and how fragile I had truly become. I have never considered myself weak. As a matter of fact, if you made me mad enough to cry, you'd better take off running because I was coming your way. That was not the case anymore. Crying had become my new normal and there weren't many other emotions. I stayed in bed most of the day. The rest of the time, I had anxiety and felt as if I were going to lose someone else close to me. My youngest son still lived at home and every time he left the house I would pace the floor frantically until he returned.

The first birthday without her was honestly a living nightmare. The weeks leading up to it were a constant rollercoaster of emotion. While visiting Neva during her final few weeks, I had asked her many times how in the world was I ever going to celebrate a birthday without her. She would just smile and tell me to "eat sushi and be forty-eight forever." Of course, her unselfish nature is what prompted that response. She knew that sushi is one of my favorite foods.

I tried to prepare myself for the big day without her. I knew that anxiety and stress were inevitable, but I tried to cope and tell myself that she was there by my side. Since Neva and I never had a birthday cake as children, I was determined to have the most beautiful cake in honor of my twin. My husband took it upon himself to design the cake and invited my sisters and children to help celebrate Neva's and my birthday.

The cake reveal left me speechless. My husband had designed a four-tier cake more beautiful than any wedding cake I'd ever seen. He included one tier for each decade Neva and I had together. The top tier was decorated with twin figures, one sporting stunning angel wings. Of course, the cake overwhelmed me with emotion but it was everything I had imagined – it was perfect! I know that I will learn to go on without her, but I will celebrate this day always wishing she were here. She will never have a birthday without a cake again and she will always be the angel on the top of it.

I have studied the effects of loss, especially related to twin loss, ever since I realized my Neva wouldn't be with me to grow old together. I knew depression was possible but didn't think it would affect me. I also didn't know it would make me feel so terribly helpless, lifeless, and with the desire to end my life. However, I know I am luckier than many who have been in my shoes before. I owe that fortune to Neva. It was she who rescued me from the darkness.

As I slept one night, Neva came to me in a dream. The dream was remarkably vivid and she was beautifully dressed. She was an angel and she came to deliver me a message. A message I will never forget. Neva gently grabbed my chin and raised my sobbing face up to hers. She (forcefully? authoritatively? firmly? gently? lovingly?) said, "Eva, lift your chin and get busy living." In this magical dream, Neva was courageous, witty, and strong again. She was no longer frail and lifeless as I had last seen her. It was the Neva I knew my whole life. I knew she meant those words and they couldn't have come at a better time. I slept peacefully the rest of the night; more peaceful than I had before I knew she was leaving me forever.

I woke the next morning with a feeling of relief. I knew she would not want to me to be this way. She would kick me in the rear, punch my arm, and probably call me a butthead if she were still alive. I decided to do exactly what she said. Being incredibly moved by her presence, I created a plan to re-establish myself and move on without her physically here. I decided to be selfish for the first time in my life; I knew I needed to discover Eva as an individual again – only now it would be as a singular soul. I looked in the mirror again. Who was I really? What did I stand for? What defines Me? What am I capable of?

I believe we all find our own way to deal with grief. Whether it is painting, writing, fitness, or picking up a new hobby, keeping busy is a way of coping with the pain and engaging our mind in something other than the sadness. I thought about all the things I had ever wanted to do in my life. Those things that I willingly set aside to raise my family. I have always loved being athletic and had a lifelong dream to compete in a figure competition. Sadly, though, I had gained 40 pounds with the stress of grief. So, there I was; I knew that getting my health back was my new mission to show Neva I was going to keep on living.

I purchased a figure competition suit over fifteen years ago and it had been hanging in my closet all those years. I always loved working out but had no idea where to start for the competitive adventure I had set my sights on. I just knew that was something I could do for myself that no one else could. My passion turned into an hourly, daily, monthly distraction. It kept my mind busy for seven intense months. Of course, the grief would find its devious way to sneak up on me. There were occasions I would be on the treadmill or lifting weights and a song would come on that broke me. I found myself allowing my body to weep but pushing harder through the workout as I sobbed.

Before I knew it, I had done it! The competition date was near and I was ready. But now what? I found myself worried that I would fall into the darkness again. What was I going to focus on after this? I constantly reminded myself of my accomplishment and the amazing journey I experienced. I imagined Neva sitting in the audience as I walked across the stage. I pushed harder the last few days before the competition.

The day arrived and I was terrified. I wasn't sure how my anxious and shy self would be able to do walk out onto the stage in a tiny bikini in front of so many strangers. I heard my name announced and stepped out from the curtain in my dazzling two-piece suit and five-inch heels. I felt it. I felt ME. THIS is who I am! Strong. Motivated. Beautiful. Singular. I had so much joy in my heart for the first time in over a year. For the first time, I allowed myself to be strong and do something for myself.

I know that Neva was with me that day as I stepped onto that stage but she let me shine. She gave me the courage that I would never have had on my own. I felt no shyness or anxiety, only bravery and power from my twin. I walked with confidence and grace, and was overjoyed to accept my second-place trophy. I know Neva would have been proud of me. She would have been proud that I allowed myself to do something for me.

As my life continues without her, I have yet to make it through a day without thinking of her and wishing she were here. I replay moments, both good and bad, and still cry myself to sleep often. Even as I sit here writing my story, tears engulf my eyes and fall down my cheeks. The true reality is that I know the pain will never completely fade. The scar on my heart is permanent. But I also know that Neva is with me every day. She loved life and would want me to continue living, to continue establishing my place, cherishing my children and grandchildren, and not letting one moment with my family be taken for granted. I want to continue living for her. For me! I may not be a complete soul, and I will forever be lacking my other half, but I know I will see her again one day.

For you, my Neva, I love you. Thank you for giving me strength, courage, and laughter . . .

Things I've Learned from Losing My Twin

* Making silly memories is not just for children.
* You can stay up late with your twin, watching movies and eating ice cream, even when you're forty-eight.
* Cuddling is never weird. It's precious and I miss it.
* You never look ugly crying when you have a reason to cry.
* You'll always have a partner-in-crime and a partner-to-fight when you are in battle . . . even when you can't see them any longer.
* She'll never know the rock that she was for me and how much I looked up to her.
* Grief, and its symptoms, are colorful and they change time and time again.
* I will never be able to pick up the phone just to chat with her.

* No matter the illness or age, I will never EVER forget her.

* I cannot live for her; I must live for myself.

* I can't rationalize or negotiate her death. It happened, it was ugly, and I cannot change it. I CAN, however, memorialize the beautiful days and memories with her.

* Any and all suicidal thoughts were only the result of my anxiety and depression. They don't control me; I can control them.

* I will forever be changed by her leaving.

* I know that she is there waiting for me to finish my journey.

* When my days are dark, I know I always have my dreams of her, and my fellow twinless twins, friends, and family.

* I work harder than ever before to live life fully again.

* The emotions of anger, shock, denial, guilt, fear, and betrayal will continue to hit with dizzying unpredictability. I know now these are a sign of moving forward through grief.

* I am half of a whole and will carry her with me every day until I see her again.

* On every August 14 I know I will, "just eat sushi and be forty-eight forever."

Double the love. Double the strength.
And ALWAYS~ Double the trouble.
I love you, Neva!

PART II

From Twins, For Twins

Daryl And Dawn

After Neva died, I searched for people like me and found the wonderful group, Twinless Twins Support Group International (TTSGI). I have made the most remarkable friends along the way. Although some may not know it, they have been the best support system for me. I have spent countless hours reading their stories, desperately seeking guidance from those who know exactly what I'm going through. The focus at TTSGI is on the similarities of loss rather than the differences, and I have found a level of support and understanding that compares to none other. We are united in our search for singularity, while never forgetting our other halves.

One special friend is Dawn Barnett. Dawn is the 2013 TTSGI Dr. Brandt Memorial award winner. This award was created in 2001 and is presented by the TTSGI Board of Directors. It is given to a member "whose contribution and dedication to helping twinless twins parallels that of the late Dr. Raymond W. Brandt," who founded TTSGI in 1987. The award honors the memory of Dr. Brandt in effort to "carry on this great man's work and life-long passion."

I am truly honored that Dawn chose to share her story with you and me. For more information on Dr. Brandt and TTSGI, please go to www.twinlesstwins.org. Dawn is also a moderator of the TTSGI Facebook page. She is one of many administrators who offer compassion and daily inspiration to all of us touched by twin loss.

"Daryl and Dawn" by Dawn Barnett

My identical twin sister, Daryl, and I were born on Dec. 10, 1947, in Norman, Oklahoma. We were the first set of twins born in the new hospital there. Daryl was the oldest by 4 minutes. As I was traveling the birth canal, the umbilical cord wrapped around my neck, but the doctors were able to get it loose without harming me. Our two uncles who were attending Oklahoma University named us, and they came every night to visit, telling everyone who would listen who we were. When we were a week old they brought a name book and informed our parents that they were going to name us before they went home that night. And they did — Daryl and Dawn. In 2007, I lost Uncle Tony to a stroke; I attended and spoke at my Uncle Bill's services a year later. Uncle Bill never had children so his nieces and nephews were quite special to him. We were very close.

The first month of our life was precarious because none of the baby formulas were working for either of us. We had a landlady who raised goats and she suggested our mother try goat's milk. She did and it worked. We gained weight and did better immediately so our father was out milking the goat — sometimes at 2:00 a.m. — after he closed his business and came home from work. He made sure we got the special milk so we could grow and be healthy. The only thing was we became so malnourished we lost all of our hair and when we got better it started growing back; mine came in faster so that was the only time people close to us could tell us apart!

Mine was growing straight up! But most people could not distinguish any differences. I also had a birthmark on my belly button and they could tell us apart by that. Otherwise, we were mirror identical. Mama often said I was more active and had a tendency to take toys away from Daryl, but she didn't mind. Daryl would just pick up another one and was happy with that. She said that we were very content babies and only cried when we were hungry or hurt. Since we were born before the days of disposable diapers, she complained of having tons of laundry and long clotheslines.

On September 27, 1948, my mother was in the hospital having just delivered my younger sister, Jackie, who was born two months premature. She knew something was up when a doctor came into her room and asked if she still lived at the same address. Mom called home to my grandmother who told her Daryl was burning up with a fever. The doctor had made a house call and said Daryl needed to go to the hospital immediately. Upon hearing the news, my mother left without the doctor's knowledge and took a cab home. I don't know how she had the strength after having just given birth that day.

Daryl had pneumonia. The Norman hospital had limited facilities for such intensive infant care so she had to be taken to Children's Hospital in Oklahoma City. A short time later I became ill with the same symptoms. At the time, the doctors weren't sure what was wrong so I was hospitalized as well since Daryl was getting sicker. Daryl continued to worsen and died on Oct. 12, 1948 at the age of ten months, 2 days. I kept improving but spent two more weeks in the hospital. I was kept so isolated I thought the nurses and doctors were my family. Since the doctors couldn't find the cause of what made us sick, they wouldn't let me be with our mother. This was hard on both of us.

Daryl died from pneumonia and a syndrome the medical profession of the time called a "weak heart." The death certificate says she died of "congestive heart failure due to hypochromic anemia severe." We now know it was a hereditary disease called Long QT Syndrome, a heart arrhythmia. In 2004, I had a heart attack precipitated by a medication I was taking which resulted in Long QT Syndrome manifesting itself in me. My heart stopped beating three times before the paramedics could stabilize it and get me to the hospital. I was in a coma for a week. The cardiologists had determined my heart and arteries were perfectly sound, the cause of the heart attack was hereditary arrhythmia. My comatose state allowed my brain to heal from the lack of oxygen. When I awoke, I was fine except for some memory loss. I was mostly inactive for an entire year. The doctors would not allow me to drive. My heart was and is perfectly fine now because I wear a pacemaker/defibrillator to ward off another arrhythmia.

Although I lost Daryl at an early age and never got to form any memories of her, the loss affected me all my life. I came home from the hospital three weeks after Daryl died to another baby. Jackie was nine months younger than I. Instead of being united with my twin, I was united with a stranger. I know that had to be very confusing to me even at that young age. Because she had two young babies to care for, my mother never actually had time to grieve Daryl's death. In 1948 when there was a death in the family, pictures were put away and the deceased were not spoken of much again. My mother practically raised my sister, Jackie and I like twins as we shared the same room, often wore clothes alike, were close to the same age so were in the same grade through 12th grade, etc. In later years I gave her a book written by a friend of mine who lost her twin to twin-to-twin transfusion and Mama told me the book "really hit a cord with her." She said she never had anyone to talk to when she lost Daryl and had to grieve in silence.

To this day, some sixty-nine years later, I still have "abandonment" issues. Whenever I moved or changed jobs, lost friends due to changes, lost dogs and relatives to death, I was devastated. Even in a crowded room, I led a lonely life. I would panic whenever I got lost, which was often. I would joke that when God made me, I wasn't equipped with a compass. It was hard for me to accept change. I looked for my twin in friends and relationships only to be disappointed because they were never the perfect partner that I had with Daryl. I had an empty feeling inside me like something was missing. It was Daryl of course. She was half of my soul, half of my being. I grew up left- and right-handed, not ambidextrous. I wrote, ate, and played tennis with my right hand. I threw, batted, and played golf left-handed. We were mirror twins and I took on her side of the characteristics.

As a youngster, I felt best with my grandparents on the farm. I would play with my collie companion, Lucky, and always had a make-believe companion. My grandmother would tell me stories of Daryl and I and that made me feel good because that kept my twin alive in my heart. She showed me our dainty little white beaded hospital bracelets in the shape of play blocks with our names on them. I also remember her showing me Daryl's obituary. My parents never talked about her because I think they never got over the grief of losing a child and I was a reminder of the one that they lost. Besides this, they had three children under the age of three to take care of. I do remember going to a place they called "the cemetery" but I was too young to understand what was going on. Then there were the times we visited relatives who I didn't know, and they would ask: "Is this the twin?"

In 1994, I became acquainted with Dr. Raymond Brandt, the founder of Twinless Twins Support Group, Int'l, after seeing him as a guest on a TV talk show. Why I have felt as I have over the years became extremely apparent to me. I called him several days later. As I got to know him, he was very consoling and understanding. I discovered that he treated every twinless twin personally. He dedicated his life and a lot of resources to the organization. I was always an overachiever.

All the twinless twins he had met were overachievers. It is as if we are fulfilling the void left by our twins.

It took me three years to finally accept Dr. Brandt's "once a twin, always a twin" belief. It happened when I went to my first TTSGI conference in 1997. It was in Chicago at the old McDonald's campus. That was truly the time my twinship journey began. I met Dr. Brandt and his bride, Miriam, in person and we became lifelong friends. I also met many twinless twins and had wonderful, caring roommates help me through that very emotional first conference. It's where I discovered: I am a twin; not I was a twin.

I was the South Central Regional Director for four years until my heart attack forced me to quit. I served on the Board of TTSGI for six years and was on the conference committee various times and have attended seventeen conferences. I was the raffle/auction chairman for many years at the conferences, and was also the moderator/admin for various social medias such as Yahoo Group, Chatline, and Facebook Group throughout the seventeen years for the organization. As Eva mentioned, I was honored to receive the coveted Dr. Brandt Award in 2013. My son, Aaron, designed the previous website 2006-2012; served as webmaster, and received an Angel Award, which is given to deserving individuals who contribute their time and efforts to the cause. I am so thankful we have such an organization for twinless twins.

I wrote this article for the Twinless Times and have a memorial outside my front door; the picture is attached hereto above:

A MEMORIAL TO DARYL

Twinless Twins, lighthouses, and seashells. What do they have in common? A fantastic connection with my identical twin sister, Daryl.

Although I lost Daryl when we were only ten months old and was not afforded the opportunity to live a life with her during these past years, I know she's been with me during all the wonderful moments and incomprehensibly terrible events of my lifetime. I underestimated how much of a "we" I was until I met Dr. Brandt. The many times he tried to tell me, "You ARE a twin, not I WAS a twin. Once a twin, always a twin," he would say. In 1997, three years after I connected with him by correspondence, I attended my first conference and therein began my twin journey. Twelve years and nine conferences later, I have come to realize Daryl has been with me every step of the way. There were many lonely times and feelings that something was missing. There was no one to talk to because everyone just couldn't understand the meaning of missing your twin. "How can you miss a twin sister you never lived with or knew?" was the response I would get when trying to tell someone how I felt. There was an incredible emptiness. Only another twinless twin can answer this question. So, comes the meaning of this memorial to my beloved Daryl. I miss her every day of my life.

TTSGI has brought the essence of her back into my life. Ever heard the saying, healing by helping? Well, I do all I can for twinless twins because this organization has helped me to heal so I can help others who have lost a twin. I have always had a passion for lighthouses and seashells. Throughout my life, I would comb whatever beach I was on — Galveston while growing up in Oklahoma. Later in my travels, I collected thousands of shells in the states of California, Texas, Alabama, Florida — including Sanibel Island, the shell capital of the world —and Hawaii, having thoughts of Daryl the whole time. Whenever I came upon a lighthouse, it fascinated me. I took photos, read stories, and painted them. I collected many calendars depicting them.

This is how Twinless Twins, lighthouses, and seashells came together in my memorial to Daryl. After retiring, my husband and I moved from Texas to Hot Springs Village, Arkansas. I was determined to do something special in this beautiful Arkansas landscape, a place I call "heaven on earth." My wonderful husband, Dan, recently surprised me with a four-foot replica of the lighthouse in West Quoddy, Maine. Last year I was fortunate to buy a stone at the Twinless Twins Toronto Conference donated by Eileen Jensen. And with our move came the buckets of shells I had collected over the years. So Voilà! Here is my memorial. I situated it right by our front doorway. All three of these things remind me of Daryl. The stone with the TTSGI logo on it is included for the obvious reason. Lighthouses project a beam of light that can symbolize hope, and my lighthouse symbolizes the everlasting hope of being reunited with Daryl when my time on earth is over. The shells are here because as I combed the beaches for them, I felt her presence and knew she was with me. I had thoughts of her during the many hours of arranging them around the lighthouse and stone and will remember her every time I enter and leave from the doorway of my house.

I share this memorial with all of you and want you to know how much each and every one of the twinless twins who I have met means to me. In addition, thank you, Dr. Brandt, for founding this remarkable organization so that we can realize the "specialness" of being a twin.

Daryl and Dawn

Charla and Carla

Finding ways to tell my story has been a transformational practice. I am growing as a person and strengthening my ability to manage my grief each day I share my life. The very beginning of this journey was impossible to imagine and I lived in a state of constant depression and denial. One of the very first people to reach out with support was Charla Haley Fitzwater. Charla immediately offered words of encouragement and hope. She made sure I was never alone in my bereavement journey. We quickly became friends through social media and found that our stories of loss are very similar. I had forty-eight years with my sister and lost her to stomach cancer. Charla had fifty-eight years with her twin sister before her loss to lung cancer. An important thing I have learned since starting this collection is the importance of sharing my story. It is not just the telling or writing it down, but knowing that what you write will be read and offer support and inspiration to others. Just like Charla has done for me.

"Charla and Carla" by Charla Haley Fitzwater

The message on my phone read, "Lung cancer. Will call when I get home. Sigh." I remember screaming in my office in Utah, understanding that things were going to change dramatically for my family. The message was from my 58-year old twin sister, a heavy smoker who lived in Tulsa, Oklahoma. A week later, on January 21, 2015, we learned how bad it was. In her words, "It's everywhere."

Quickly, I rallied my family and we all converged on Tulsa for a weekend of celebrating just being together. We laughed and cried and all the while my sister's carefully chosen words were, "It'll be fine." After everyone left, I stayed another week or so, taking my twin to her first two radiation appointments and spending time with her husband, Mike, daughter, Jenison and son, Michael. She was positive, upbeat, and told everyone, "I'm really healthy except for the cancer." And, she'd chuckle, refusing to let anyone give her a prognosis. She said it wouldn't change anything and it didn't.

I returned to my home in Salt Lake City, knowing that I'd be back in Oklahoma in mid-March as we celebrated our sweet mother's 93rd birthday. What I didn't anticipate was that after three weeks of radiation, my sister had lost 20 pounds and wasn't eating or drinking much because getting the radiation so close to her esophagus had made swallowing painful. The following Monday, she was admitted to the hospital.

Two days later, she started having trouble breathing and was moved to ICU. Once again, I boarded a plane to be by her side. I spent nearly two weeks in Tulsa, going to the hospital every day, trying to encourage her to eat and getting her husband to bring her two scoops of lemon custard ice cream from Baskin Robbins, a childhood favorite. She started chemotherapy while in ICU, and on a joyful Friday, her oxygen levels were better and she was moved out of ICU to a regular room. The next few days were lovely, with Carla feeling better each day. Sunday night, I helped the nurses take her into a special room for a shower. She was weak and needed a lot of help washing her hair and her body, but she said it felt "heavenly." Monday was another good day and I decided it was safe to fly home. Tuesday, I boarded a plane back to Salt Lake City.

Unfortunately, our optimism was short-lived. Wednesday morning, I received texts from Carla's family that her oxygen levels were once again a problem and they were going to move her back to ICU. A few minutes later, following assurances to the family that she hadn't "taken a turn for the worse," they gave Carla some platelets and decided not to move her.

On Friday, I received a text from Carla's family saying the oncologist had been in and that the tumors were smaller and things were looking up. We were joyful! I went into the weekend feeling optimistic that we'd have a little more time together.

My phone rang early Sunday morning. It was my brother-in-law, Mike, telling me that Carla's oxygen levels were bad again and they wanted to put her on a ventilator. Mike and I had already had that conversation during my earlier visit and we had all agreed. None of us wanted her to live that way, even if it were only for a short time. I hung up after telling him I'd book a flight and be there as soon as I could.

The words on the computer blurred as I booked a Delta flight that would arrive in Tulsa at 5 p.m. I called Mike's phone and told him when my flight would land and asked to speak to my sister. I told her, "I'll be there at 5. Don't go anywhere!" She talked for what seemed like a long time; unfortunately, with the oxygen mask she was wearing, I couldn't understand her. When she stopped talking, I said, "Honey, I'm so sorry. I have no idea what you said. I love you and I'll be there at 5. Please, don't go anywhere."

I threw stuff into a suitcase and included some skirts that would be suitable for a funeral. My son and his girlfriend took me to the airport and somehow, I managed to hold it together fairly well. Once I was checked in and through security, I realized I had the beginnings of a headache. Knowing I was in for a long, heartbreaking day, I bought some Tylenol and went into the bathroom to take some. I tried to open the package and completely lost it! My heart was breaking and the poor Delta flight attendants who were in the lady's room could tell as I tried to explain through the tears that I was heading to Tulsa to bid a final farewell to my twin sister. One of them opened the pills for me and another just held me as I sobbed. As I pulled myself together, I thanked them profusely and they each said they would pray for me and Carla's family.

Anxiously, I boarded my flight, praying that Carla would hang on until I got there. Mike picked me up at the airport and said she was still hanging on, but the hospice nurse wanted to talk to us as soon as we got to the hospital.

I couldn't get out of the car fast enough and Mike and I rushed through the hospital, wondering what we'd find when we reached Carla's room. I kept hoping that ours would be one of those twin stories where the arrival of the missing twin turned everything around. Sadly, it was not to be.

When we got to the room, I rushed to her side, told her I loved her and kissed her on the forehead. Even though the cumbersome oxygen mask was still on, I could make out her muffled words as she responded, "I love you, too."

The hospice nurse ushered us to a nearby sitting room and explained that Carla was unlikely to live through the night. Her recommendation was for us to go back in to Carla's room, and ask her whether she was ready to take the uncomfortable oxygen mask off. She explained that everyone hates the mask and that the simple cannula delivering oxygen was much more comfortable and would allow us to hear her speak.

We tearfully agreed, thanked her and went back to Carla's room. Mike walked to the head of the bed and asked her if she would like to take the mask off. She opened her eyes, smiled and nodded her head. Gently, Mike helped her lift her head and gingerly removed the mask. He and the nurse replaced it with the cannula and she said, "Better."

Our group was large, consisting of me, our stepmom, our younger sister, Cheri, her husband, Wayne, and daughter, Alyssa, Jenison, and Mike. We went around the room and each of us told her we loved her. She responded to each one of us saying, "I love you, too." The chaplain said a prayer and then asked whether she liked music. Her daughter and I looked at each other and smiled, wondering why we hadn't thought of that. Jenison and I in unison said, "September by Earth, Wind, and Fire." Jenison found it on her phone and the joyous sounds filled the room. We listened to some of Carla's favorite songs, as we cried, laughed, and shared stories while she quietly slipped away, me holding one hand and Mike holding the other. Before she took her last breath, I said, "Don't be a stranger." It was all over just before 8 p.m. It was March 8, 2015.

The rest of that night and the next day were a blur as we went to a funeral home that had been recommended to Mike. We were less than impressed by the service feeling as if we were dealing with used car salesmen and shocked by the huge price tag they were asking. Mike excused himself and placed a phone call to a family friend who was in charge of planning funerals for a Methodist church in Tulsa. She said she'd call us back with information for a more affordable option. We made our excuses and left.

The next morning was a completely different experience as Carla led us through the day. First, we went to the funeral home that had been highly recommended by our family friend, where a funeral planner greeted us at the door and showed us to a table to begin planning the service. As I sat down, Carla let me know we were in the right place when I noticed the program facing me was a lovely print of purple flowers and yellow butterflies. Carla's favorite colors and two of her favorite things! I picked it up and showed Mike and Jenison and we all chuckled through our tears. She made that choice really easy!

The program chosen, Mike let the mortician know about two songs he wanted played for the funeral. And he told Jenison and me that we could pick the third song. We indicated we'd think about it and get back to the funeral planner as soon as we had made our third choice.

Then, the planner ushered us to another room where we picked out the casket, a lovely silvery blue color. He indicated that they had a florist they liked to recommend, one who provided lovely arrangements for about half the going rate. He gave us a name and address and we left for our next destination, all the while talking about how different this day was starting than the day before.

When we found the address, we all laughed. As we pulled into the driveway, we were greeted by the sight of a VW beetle, painted red with black polka dots to look like a ladybug. (Yep, another one of Carla's favorite things!) As we opened the door, a cat ran into the business and we walked up to the counter staffed by a lovely woman, dressed all in purple. (Carla's favorite color!) I asked about the cat, and she said the cat actually lived at the business and that the owner loved rescuing strays. Another cause near and dear to Carla's heart! We picked out the flowers using lots of purple and yellow blooms and thanked the sales clerk for her kindness. Smiling as we left, the three of us went to our next destination, the business office for a cemetery that our family friend had also suggested.

As we arrived at Green Acres Memorial Gardens, Jenison and I commented on how much Carla would love the idea of being buried at Green Acres. The TV show of the same name held fond memories for Carla and me. We all giggled as the three of us started singing the show's theme song! (Something Carla would have joined us in.) Once we found the appropriate office, we walked in and felt as if we'd stepped back in time. The woman who greeted us was in her 70s, wearing all lime green and there wasn't a single computer in the place! As we talked, we discovered that Jenison and Michael had attended grade school with her grandchildren. (Thanks again, Carla!) She explained how theirs was a family business, very small and that the cemetery was just a few miles out of town. She placed a call to her brother to let him know to expect us.

We thanked her for helping us through such a difficult time with quiet compassion and Jenison and I both felt compelled to give her a hug. Despite our heavy hearts, we were all touched by the empathy expressed by the incredible people we were meeting during our time of grief.

The drive to the cemetery was filled with a discussion of awe and amazement at the treatment we were receiving from some lovely, very special people. And, we also talked about a memory video one of Carla's friends was going to make for us, free of charge, in her honor. (What a lovely, heartfelt gesture.) We chose the songs September by Earth, Wind, and Fire, Abba's Dancing Queen, and Do You Hear the People Sing from Les Misérables, some of Carla's favorite songs. As we pulled off the highway on to a dirt road, we could see the quaint, small cemetery just around the corner. Even though it was just off the highway, it had a lovely, peaceful feeling.

We pulled up to the lone pickup sitting in the center of the cemetery and were greeted by a friendly, very down-to-earth older gentleman, who welcomed us to Green Acres. We asked which plots were available and he explained that if there wasn't a marker, it was probably open. Mike and I started walking across the cemetery, each of us drawn to a lovely plot near the outer edge with a nearby tree. We asked whether it was open, and he called his sister back at the office, since she had the maps with the open plots marked.

Following a short conversation with his sister, he said that particular plot wasn't open, but that the plots just above it were. Then, he asked whether we remembered Tulsa's legendary meteorologist Don Woods and his beloved weather-ready cartoon character, Gusty. Jenison and Mike both exclaimed he was Carla's favorite! So, we chose the plot for Carla that is just above Don and Mike will eventually be next to her above Don's wife.

We thanked him and walked back to Mike's car. He started the engine, turned on the radio, and we all gasped when the song playing on the radio was Dancing Queen by Abba! We all looked upward and said, "Yep, she's with us! Love you!"

Mike maneuvered the car out of the cemetery and as we approached the end of the dirt road to make our way back onto the highway, he said that would be the only bad part, crossing oncoming highway traffic to get back onto the side of the road to head home. He stopped at the stop sign and we all looked both ways and laughed. The road was completely clear of traffic! "Thank you, Carla," we all yelled!

Then, Jenison and I started talking about that third song. What should we choose? Just then the song changed on the radio and she and I looked at each other saying, "That's perfect," as we heard the beginning strains of Billy Joel's Only the Good Die Young. Thanks, Carla!

Since then, she's been with each one of us many times and we are always grateful for the reminder that where there is deep grief there was great love!

Charla and Carla
June 2014

Stories of Early Twin Loss

According to the CDC, the percentages of twin births have soared almost 76% since 1980 due to advancing technologies. This miraculous increase also generates an increase in potential high-risk pregnancies and twin losses. Studies show that early twin loss can be caused by many reasons, including Vanishing Twin Syndrome, Sudden Infant Death, sickness, and accidental death. Early twin loss has been known to greatly affect the surviving twin. There is overwhelming suggestion that surviving twins tend to suffer from personality disorders such as abandonment, fear of rejection, feelings of being alone and different from other people, and feelings of incompleteness. Studies and research go on to suggest that these manifestations may not be a mental health personality disorder, but a rational, intelligent response to a rather unusual pre-birth or early loss situation.

A British online news article "Lose you twin, live half a life," authored by David Cohen of The Independent, unknowingly introduced me to two renowned researchers of twin loss. Joan Woodward, an author, psychotherapist and fellow twinless twin, founded the Lone Twin Network in the late-1980s as a support group for lone twins to share their experiences and grief with one another. During this time, according to the network's origins at lonetwinnetwork.org, Joan interviewed over two hundred lone twins to research their responses to the death of their twins. Her results revealed the most distressed of the lone twins were often those who lost their twin at birth. "It seems that memory occurs in the fetus at around six months and that for the last three months in the womb, the twins definitely have an awareness of each other's existence, but as far as we know, memory may occur earlier."

Cohen brought forth another study by Alessandra Piontelli, a professor who tracked the relationship of twins from womb to childhood. "What she found, as she watched them on ultrasound scans, was that she could categorize their relationship in the womb as the playful pair, the cuddly pair, or the hostile pair and that the relationship they developed after birth corresponded exactly to the relationship begun in the womb. No scientific evidence exists that establishes when bonding begins, personal testimonies of lone twins suggests strongly that the impact of bonding in the womb is profound and significant."

Through ongoing research efforts by people like Joan and Alessandra, and through fellow authors sharing their stories like David Cohen, we know it is evident that twins who were separated in the womb, or early in life, will experience a sense of loss as they grow older.

A friend of mine, Crystal Hewell, lost her twin sister, Lacie, due to Twin to Twin Transfusion Syndrome. Twin-twin transfusion syndrome (TTTS) is a rare and serious condition that can occur in pregnancies when identical twins share a placenta. Abnormal blood vessel connections form in the placenta and allow blood to flow unevenly between the babies. Here is Crystal's story.

"Crystal & Lacie" by Crystal Hewell

I lost my twin in the first hours of our life. I never knew her, consciously. I often find myself wondering what our bond was like in utero. My feelings about my twin lie in the abstract of what-ifs and more questions than answers. I wonder if her face would still look like mine these thirty-two years later. I wonder what her personality would be like in comparison to mine, would she have been the yin to my yang. Sometimes my thoughts drift more toward the unknown like an unbalanced pendulum, would she have been my other half, would we have had that "twin thing" and would we have known what the other was thinking and feeling? The pendulum swings one way, but never fully swings back. I wonder if we would be close, if we would have fought like opposites, or would we have known all the right things to say, being carbon copies of each other, after all.

I often find myself more struck by the biology of it all, the same DNA, the very cell structure of ourselves existing in another living, breathing human being, walking around the Earth, able to live completely separate lives while being a mirror image of each other. Step back and think about the oddness of that, the queer ability to have two souls in the same body just living out our wildest dreams and making our mark on the world. Identical twins have jobs, have significant others, have kids, and are the same in every way except the thoughts and desires in our own brains. That's about as abstract as it can get without being in some strange mirror dimension that physicists can only theorize about.

TTTS or Twin to Twin Transfusion Syndrome is how I lost my twin. It happens only with identical twins, or higher multiple pregnancies. In our case, I was the "donor twin." I was born very small at only two pounds. Current statistics state I would have been 20% smaller than she was. We were due in August, but born eight weeks early on June 24th. The lower the gestational age, the greater risk for adverse outcomes due to lessened blood supply and many other health factors. And this was in the late 80's, before a TTTS diagnosis was correctable. Our TTTS was undiagnosed throughout my mother's pregnancy.

To say the numbers were against us is an understatement. I was in an incubator for the first three months of my life. The fact that the doctors kept me alive and I was released with no neurological or bodily damage (the doctors did not give my Mom a good outcome to look forward to) is absolutely astonishing. How I ended up the one here is like looking into a mirror with another mirror behind you. Infinite chances. I cannot help but think that my fruitful life has something to do with her tether to me, in the womb and in the afterlife.

Here I am. Thirty-two years later without her, and yet still infinitely connected to her, always wondering. The one thing I'm certain of about our relationship is that I'm eternally grateful for her existence however brief it was.

-Crystal Hewell, twin to Lacie

Similar to Crystal's, here is another beautiful story by Anjy Lobelia Roemelt. She lost her twin in utero over fifty years ago.

"Anjy & Enjy" by Anjy Lobelia Roemelt

"You can't miss what you never had!"

It's the most common reaction an early-loss twinless twin gets when we first tell our story to others. You can't miss your twin, you never knew him/her.

This is true. You don't miss what you never had. I know that from experience.

I was born with my nose slightly more narrow than comfortable for breathing through it. I never knew that until some years ago - I was well into my forties when a doctor examined me and casually mentioned, "Your nose is very narrow. You must have trouble breathing through it." I was like, "Oh. Yeah. Right. Probably." The truth is, I never thought about that before. My way of breathing was just my way of breathing. It's only in moments like last weekend when I swallowed a fly while riding my bike with my mouth open (for breathing) I realize I REALLY can't breathe too well through my nose. But I don't miss doing it because I never did it.

I do miss my twin, though.

I have always missed him. I have been talking to an invisible brother as long as I can remember. People used to smile at my "imaginary brother" at age four. Now, at age 47, I am going to psychotherapy, of course, still talking to him. But inside me nothing has changed. He's still there. A silent, absent presence - if such a thing is possible.

It's true - you can't miss what you never had. The fact that I miss you so much, Enjy, is proof I had you.

-Anjy Lobelia Roemelt, twin to Enjy

If you would like to learn more about the Lone Twin Network, you can find them online at https://lonetwinnetwork.org.uk.

The Lone Twin Network is a voluntary group that offers support to those affected by loss at birth, in childhood, and during adulthood. The group has members from all over the world and through meetings and personal contact, aims to offer a friendly and comfortable environment in which to talk openly and honestly about how it feels to be without your twin.

As a mother, my biggest fear in life has been that of losing a child. Through my research on early twin loss, I found numerous stories from parents who lost one of their twins in utero, at birth, or in the early stages of life. I want to share with you a remarkable story about early twin loss from a mother's perspective. Her story of loss and honoring her sweet twin really touched my heart.

"My Later Abortion of One Twin Saved Our Daughter's Life. This Is Our Story."
by Darla Barer

The introduction of state- and federal-level abortion restriction legislation, as well as the utterly false narrative of late-term abortions spun during the presidential debates last year, have ignited the pro/anti-choice debate again and sent lawmakers into a frenzy to introduce many restrictive measures. H.R.586, essentially a federal "personhood" and "heartbeat" bill, and Texas's "wrongful birth" S.B.25 are just two of the federal- and state-level bills introduced to restrict abortions. I want you to know the faces of the issue. I am the issue. My husband is the issue. Our daughters are the issue.

We struggled to get pregnant. When other treatments failed, we decided to travel from our home in Texas to the Czech Republic to use donor eggs. We transferred our only two embryos and later found we were having twin girls. We got to know them, and we loved them fiercely: our little diva, Olivia, and camera-shy cuddle bug, Catherine.

I remember being anxious to get to and through our 20-week scan in June because, with twins, the 20-week mark is as safe as you can get in terms of miscarriage risks. Afterward, the doctor took over an hour to come in. He asked me to sit down next to my husband before telling us that Catherine had a number of issues.

The encephalocele (a neural tube defect) was the most dire. They occur in about 1 in 13,000 live births each year, and only one in five babies diagnosed with an encephalocele in utero survive to delivery. She was a couple of weeks behind in growth, had a large cleft lip/palate that was making it impossible for her to swallow amniotic fluid and regulate her sac size, and she showed signs of fused digits.

Our obstetrician told us if she made it through delivery, she would suffer greatly. He referred us to a specialist, the only one in town he knew of who would perform the unthinkable, should we need it.

That specialist called us directly that evening. He wanted to do his own imaging but described her prognosis as "grim." That weekend is a blur, but I know we cried and did everything we could to distract ourselves. The specialist's scan confirmed the OB's suspicions, plus we were told her cerebellum was underdeveloped and that her sac was growing too much, putting Olivia in danger.

We opted for an amniocentesis, but while we waited for those results, we visited another specialist in Houston. He confirmed previous findings, labeled her small head size "microcephaly," had trouble even finding her cerebellum, and noted that the midline of her brain was shifted, indicating "severe disorganization," a phrase that will stick with me forever. The cleft was the width of an adult pinkie finger. The encephalocele was open and brain matter was being leached out.

Our doctors counseled us throughout the ordeal. If we carried to term, we would likely deliver early. If Catherine survived delivery, she would face a barrage of surgeries, starting with removing the encephalocele and placing her brain tissue back inside her skull. She would be severely disabled if she wasn't a vegetable. And we didn't know what an early delivery would mean for Olivia.

Our other option was to terminate half of the pregnancy. Catherine's death would likely mean a safe and healthy remaining pregnancy with Olivia.

On June 22, we saw and heard Cate one last time — she danced for us. And then the doctor injected a medication into Cate's heart. When they checked for a heartbeat thirty minutes later, the silence was deafening. When they found Olivia's strong beating heart, we cried for her survival and for Cate's loss, our loss, Olivia's loss.

We took our daughter's pain and suffering upon ourselves. She passed away peacefully, feeling my love and hearing my heartbeat. This wasn't a choice of convenience, and she wasn't unwanted. It will always hurt that we can't have her. But Olivia was wanted too. And we believe that quality of life is just as important as a beating heart.

Darla continued her letter by stating she was forever changed and a piece of her will always be missing.

"I ask for compassion for all the families who shoulder this burden for the rest of eternity. Never think that we went into this with eyes closed or made our decision lightly. I promise you we did not."

Although Darla's story may be tough for people to read and understand, I admire her for making that tough decision, but I admire her most for her desire to honor her sweet twin.

"She's 18 months now, and from day one, we always talk about her "sissy" and how she's watching over her and her brother. I have a tattoo to honor the girls. For their first birthday, we incorporated Cate in little ways, and I hope to continue to do so. We kept a box of some of Cate's things (the matching outfits, a blanket my mother-in-law made for her, and things the hospital gave to us), and I hope to give that to Olivia one day if she wants it. We never hide the fact that we should be a family of five instead of the four that we are."

After reading Darla's story I couldn't help but wonder if my mother really knew what a precious gift she had. We had a childhood filled with turmoil and I wonder if she was just too busy trying to survive. I once posted in my bereavement group asking twinless twins if their mothers showed any identifiable emotion or had any real insight on the twin-bond between their babies. I wanted to understand the maternal behavior, something that I could relate to personally. A young lady named Ashley Wood responded:

> "I'm actually a twinless twin mom. My sweet baby, Brylex, turned two on April 14; his twin sister, Alonna, was stillborn. I can guarantee you she knew how special it was. I miss my daughter every second of every day, and I feel like it's my fault that he doesn't get to grow up with his sister. It crushes me to think he should have his other half here with him."

Ashley continued to comment on my appreciation for her honoring her unborn twin:

> "I wouldn't have it any other way. Just because she is not living doesn't mean I'm not incredibly proud of her and honored to be her mother. I want the world to know about her and to remember her."

The last time I saw my mom she was dying. I was on my way back to be with Neva, and I believe that part of me must have been in shock or denial that my mom was dying too. While talking to her that last time, she gently touched my arm and tearfully told me that she had done the best she could to be our mother. Her touch was gentle and sincere. My mother wanted and needed me to understand. Hearing from people like Darla and Ashely made me realize that my mother appreciated her twins and loved us in her own way. She really did do the best that she could.

PART III

Comfort & Resources

Grief Has No Time Limit

When you lose someone you love, there is no magical date or set timeframe offering eternal relief and ongoing happiness. There is no enchanted morning you wake up to find your sadness has suddenly disappeared. Quite frankly, there are some mornings you wake up to find your sadness is even stronger than the days and weeks before. For the most part, though, the grieving process becomes more manageable with time, resources and outlets to assist in your recovery.

Grief is such a complex understanding and we are all affected by it very differently. By sharing these personal stories of twin loss, I hope you have found a glimmer of hope from others who have experienced similar feelings to you. Hindsight can be another's foresight, right? I also hope to bring you realization and comfort knowing that you aren't alone. Sometimes, all we need to power through a difficult time is to find a common denominator where people really understand what we're going through.

For me, the first year after Neva's death followed what some professionals call the "short-term grief period." It was a year filled with depression, suicidal thoughts, physical pain, and illness. The mirror was a constant reminder of the person I had lost. I remember the first time I broke down in public. I was at the grocery store and noticed the cashier's name was Eva, like mine. I engaged in conversation about our shared name and the origins of our names. I told her I was named after my grandmother and how I had a twin sister. Without a thought, I said, "Her name was Neva." My heart instantly stopped for a moment as I realized the words that came out of my mouth. I just said had and was. I felt like someone squeezed the life from my heart and soul, and I broke down right there in front of the woman who shared my name.

I look back at that moment today and realize I was growing from my loss. My twin, the half to our whole, would want me to move on while carrying her life, love, and memories with me. I am learning to live each day thinking of her and the good moments we shared. Whenever the pain and sadness creep up, I reflect on real memories that were fun and loving. Although her final days are tough to re-live, they are important to remember as well. I had never experienced death of a loved one. I had never seen what the end of life looked like. All the stages of eminent death are traumatizing. Oddly enough, though, I was thankful to be with her at the end of her life sharing those last precious moments. I got to share her first words and her last words.

Grief comes in waves. You will go for days, weeks, and even years feeling okay and then suddenly it hits you like a million pounds of rock. Know that this is completely normal and it doesn't mean you are relapsing in your grief process. Embrace those feelings – allow yourself to feel sadness, for it is just as normal as happiness. We don't always need a reason to feel low, sometimes it's just how we feel. Grieving allows us to embrace those feelings, explore them, and let go of them.

If you find yourself falling into a dark place, know that this is normal, too. Depression is painful for you and your loved ones. I'm happy to hear people admit to this terrible aspect of grief because that means they are looking for support and want to move forward. Don't keep quiet! Whether it's purchasing this book, engaging in online message boards, or seeking professional help, I know it takes courage to fight against the feeling of hopelessness, but you can do it. Pat yourself on the back for taking steps to pick yourself up and create a better life, to celebrate life. Acknowledging you've hit this point and admitting to it are very difficult tasks; I can honestly relate to. Six months after Neva's death I was in that place. I would have taken my own life had I not feared my children would find me that way. That may be hard to read but it is the truth. Depression is a very real thing that affects very real people.

I still battle with my own depression. I know I've made positive strides and I'm proud of myself for them. Trust me, it's not easy at all. I really, really know. Just getting out of bed can seem to take every ounce of energy. Removing the continuous negative thoughts and feelings is like lifting an anchor. You can lift this anchor by making a change . . . a big change. What do I recommend?

SHARE. Sharing your story can allow you to practice courage and expel feelings that are bottled inside. It's uncomfortable admitting to others your failures, struggles, and moments of weakness, but being open to moments of vulnerability is surprisingly gratifying. Fear and grief is something we all experience but publicly acknowledging your hardships is frightening, I know. Even more frightening is admitting your personal failures and mistakes.

My first few months after Neva died I researched social media groups, mainly lurking in the background. It's okay to lurk; you don't have to be actively engaged at first. After a while, I grew comfortable with the people I read about and felt like commenting and sharing my own story. The relief was gratifying and really started my journey to a better place. Find the inner strength to discover yourself as an individual and then lean on others who have experienced the same grief as you. We must fill the space for each other and pick up the broken pieces to carry each other through the darkness.

WALK. Start your day, every day, by taking a walk. Try to do so in the morning or afternoon when the sun is shining. Remove the distraction of your phone and absorb the beauty around you. The sky sure is blue. The foliage is a remarkable color this time of year. The neighbor kids are awfully sweet playing with each other. By physically removing yourself from that dark place, your mind will support you and offer natural relief, more oxygen and energy.

POSITIVELY REFLECT. Try to keep a gratitude journal. A gratitude journal has become one of the most powerful and well-researched positive psychology interventions out there. People who practice gratitude are predominantly happy and easygoing because they tend to find the positive in most negative situations. It's often when we need gratitude the most that it's difficult to find. When you're overcome with grief, sadness, anxiety or anger, it's hard to see what's going right in your life. Getting in the habit of keeping a gratitude journal is an excellent way to ensure you experience the benefits of gratitude when you need it most. What are you grateful for? Write it down daily.

I also wrote what I call my "memorial stones" in my journal. Imagine having a stone for every major event in your life. I had one for the birth of each of my children, the day I got married, the day the Lord saved me. I look at them with gratitude and love when I need a boost.

Know that there is a part of you that wants to be happy, that still holds hope. The more you keep active and incorporate little changes each day, the more confidence and evidence you will find to convince you that you can move forward.

I would like to share an essay with you from Rod Cowan. Rod is a fellow twinless twin. When Rod wrote this essay, it had been eighteen years since he lost his twin brother, Ron. He is an example of grief having no limit.

"Eighteen years" by Rod Cowan

In the last eighteen years I have had too much loss. I lost you, Ron, which was of course the worst loss. I've lost a wife and now it appears I've lost my beautiful daughters.

Ron, I have been in more hospitals than I can remember. I think eight maybe. I've tried to join you at least that many times.

It isn't until the last few months that I realized all that I have lost is not lost at all. I have a perfect wife! I will see you again so you aren't lost at all. You finally just got to sleep as much as you wanted. I am now happy for you. I know I will be the first thing you see when you wake and I'll show you what a perfect world you have woken up in.

My wife, my queen, will be right beside me. You will get to meet her and I know you will love her like I do. We will go and find my girls so you can meet them too. They are absolutely beautiful! I can't wait for you to see them. It is incredible to me that all the loss I felt I now know isn't loss. This fat body I'm in and this depression I suffer from is only temporary. I never needed as much sleep as you did so I'm going to keep fighting to be the best person I can be. You will be so surprised. I'm proud of you for being the best person you can be! We both got sober six months before you died. I must admit I went way off the sober train after you died but I'm back on it comfortably and I like it. My wife makes me feel so strong and handsome. I really can't wait for you to meet her. I have hundreds of other twins who I have met because of you. I can't wait for you to meet them either.

I got a little long winded but it has been eighteen years. I want you to know I am doing well and I'm going to make it. Emily will keep me laughing and full until it's time for you to wake up. I love you so much, Ron! I know you are sleeping well. You better be ready to get up and you better be nice about it. Maybe you'll get a jelly doughnut and a big hug, baby. I love you so much, Ron!

Rod continues to write to Ron on every birthday and on every anniversary of Ron's death. Maybe this is Rod's way of "sharing" through his blog post. He journals other fond memories to positively reflect on his life with Ron and help him through this difficult journey without his twin.

Always remember to be kind to yourself. If you're having a low few days, take care of yourself. It's all about strengthening that willpower deep inside. Take your time to grieve no matter how long it takes. Your loved one would want you to lift your head up and get busy living.

Getting Help

Sometimes our feelings can be a bit overwhelming. One of the most courageous acts you can do in times of grief is to seek help! You should never be ashamed to find professional help. Your family physician or general practitioner may be able to refer you to a mental health professional, or you can always ask your fellow support systems. Trained counselors and health professionals offer both individual and group counseling that can guide you to relief. Social networks can also help control your grief, and many people find relief in the form of peer groups.

I have a dear friend who is a grief support counselor. We were friends well before her chosen profession and, since my Neva died, I have leaned on her for more than just a friendly ear. Her expertise and passion has offered relief from things I didn't know had hurt me so badly. I love how our conversations always start out with Carolyn asking how I am doing, and sincerely wanting to know the answer. I quickly find myself asking about her day and new events in her life, but she is prompt to stop my diversion and reinforces my focus on my feelings and what's hurting underneath.

Carolyn has graciously offered to provide support by answering some commonly asked questions I've found in the Twinless Twins Support Group.

First let me introduce her. Carolyn J. Burleson is a Licensed Professional Counselor, Licensed Chemical Dependency Counselor, a Certified Clinical Trauma Professional, and a Master Addiction Counselor. She earned a bachelor's degree in Psychology and Criminal Justice from Texas Woman's University, a Master's degree in Criminal Justice from Tarleton State University, and a Master's degree in counseling from Southern Methodist University. She is currently pursuing a PhD in counselor education and supervision.

One of Carolyn's many certifications is in clinical trauma and she has several specialties, but her passion for grief recovery has led her to dedicate a portion of her practice to Twin Loss.

The following questions are those I have asked myself in trying to understand my grief.

"I don't think I'll ever get over the death of my twin. What do you suggest I do?"

The pain from twin loss can seem unbearable and intolerable and often leads to feelings of hopelessness regarding the healing process. The bond of twins begins in the womb, so losing someone you've been bonded with since before birth presents a unique and difficult bereavement process. You went through all your developmental stages with your twin, knowing each other to the point of finishing each other's sentences and knowing something was wrong with your twin as soon as it was happening. Your twin is the one person you could always trust and know that they would understand you. Once your twin is gone, you must grieve the loss of the most important part of your life, essentially the loss of yourself.

You may hurt so much that you want to crawl into a dark place and isolate yourself from everyone. Isolation leads to loneliness, which interrupts the grieving and healing process. Isolation impedes healing, which can make the healing and grieving process last longer. It is also important to accept that you can never be the same after the loss of a twin. Twins are connected to the point that losing a twin makes you feel like part of you is missing because it is! You can, however, eventually move forward and re-engage in life.

The first part of healing from twin loss is acknowledging the significance of the loss of your twin, and how that loss has affected you. You've probably relied on your twin for a lot of your life, so feeling desperately alone creates extreme pain. Acknowledging the depth of twin loss is crucial to receiving the support you need. If you don't recognize the full experience of your loss, you may feel that you "should" be better and that you don't deserve to feel grief for as long as you have.

To feel better, you must allow yourself to go through the pain of loss. In general, humans tend to steer clear of anything that causes pain. When you lose a twin, it is a seemingly unmanageable pain, and you will probably want to do something to stop it, stuff it down, or cover it up. But, you must go through the pain to heal from it. There is no getting around the pain. Talk about your twin, even when it is painful. Focus on the positive memories and journal as you remember different events you experienced together. Preserving their memory will help you through the pain, and is a good distraction from the thoughts that your twin is gone from the physical world.

You can move through the pain and re-engage in life in various ways. Some people find it helpful to journal, talk to others who have lost a twin, seek professional help, attend support groups, or find information such as on the Twinless Twins website. Unfortunately, there is not much research on the loss of a twin, and many professional therapists are not knowledgeable about the different grief associated with losing a twin versus losing a non-twin sibling. It is important to find a professional who specializes in complicated grief and if possible, find someone who has experience with twin loss. You can also refer the professional to websites related to twin loss, such as Twinless Twins. Until my best friend lost a twin, I did not know about the complicated grief associated with losing a twin. Since Neva's death, I have scoured for information regarding twin loss, and have been challenged to find resources for therapists such as myself to learn more about twin loss.

Part of the healing process is also finding a new identity. Your identity has been intertwined with your twin, so you now must deal with the loss of your twin while trying to figure out what the new you will be. For some, it is even hard to look in the mirror because your reflection is a reminder that you are alone. Losing our sense of self is a grieving process of its own. Understand that the feeling of "Who am I now?" is completely normal. Sometimes doing something in honor of your twin, such as being willing to seek professional help or achieving a goal will help you heal from the loss of your twin. Setting a goal for something you would never do before the loss of your twin can also help you find a separate identity.

"I feel suicidal. How can I live without my twin? I can't go on."

What you are feeling is a normal part of twin loss. Unfortunately, many twins feel suicidal after the loss of their twin. Although suicidal thoughts can be a normal part of complicated grief, please do not ignore them and think they will go away on their own. The most important thing you can do is express your suicide concerns immediately. If you are actively suicidal, meaning you have a plan for suicide, immediately call 911 or go to your nearest emergency room. If you are having suicidal thoughts without the intent of completing suicide or you have not started the planning phase of suicide, please immediately seek the assistance of a mental health professional.

The healing process of losing a twin is unique to any other loss. Many mental health professionals are unaware of the complex grief that occurs after the loss of a twin. It is important to find a therapist who specializes in grief, preferably specializing in complex grief. You are probably going through waves of emotion, including denial, depression, anger, despair, and guilt. You may also feel survivor's guilt, which is the feeling that it should have been you who died instead of your twin. Survivor's guilt can lead to suicidal thoughts because the guilt seems unbearable at times. Also, it is important to recognize that each person experiences the death of a twin deeply, and the key to overcoming suicidal thoughts is recognizing that your feelings are valid and that you must seek professional assistance immediately.

The American Foundation for Suicide Prevention has a list of signs and symptoms, along with resources for what to do in the case of suicidal thoughts (https://afsp.org/about-suicide/risk-factors-and-warning-signs/). The National Suicide Prevention Hotline is 1-800-273-8255 and is available 24 hours a day. And remember, please call 911 or go to your nearest emergency room if you feel that you are in danger of hurting or killing yourself or someone else. There is no shame in asking for help, even if it feels that way to you now.

"My doctor and family want me to take medication, and I don't want to. What should I tell them?"

When someone you love is hurting, it is normal for others to want a "quick fix." It is difficult to watch someone you love in immense pain. The other part of this is that because the depth of twin loss is difficult to understand unless you've been through it, people often think you should be done grieving before you've even begun the full healing process. When you haven't gotten over it soon enough for others, some people may get scared and want you to take medication. Also, people experiencing the loss of a twin can have quickly fluctuating behavior. For example, one moment you might be laughing about a positive memory with your twin and the next moment you may be sobbing uncontrollably or lashing out at someone who was trying to help. When others see the rapid changes in behavior, they may think you need medication to control the changes.

Typically, doctors follow the medical model. The medical model assumes that behavior that seems abnormal is the result of a physical problem that relates to a medical issue. Through the medical model, doctors typically treat medical problems with medication. So, if you go to a psychiatrist or a medical doctor, they will likely try to prescribe you medication because that is the approach of most physicians. I tell you this because it is important to understand that the doctors and others are trying to help in the way they know how. Your feelings of frustration regarding not wanting to take medication are also valid. Some people's sadness becomes so deep that they need to take medication to function and move through the healing process. There is no shame or guilt in taking medication, but there is also no requirement that everyone who loses a twin needs medication to heal.

You have the right to decline medication. Be careful to evaluate if you are refusing medication as a form of punishing yourself. Some people feel that they have done something wrong or don't deserve to live after the loss of a twin, so you want to make sure you are not inflicting pain on yourself by refusing help.

To decline medication, you can kindly explain that you appreciate that they love you and want to help you, but that you want to work through this grief without medication. Sometimes practicing what you want to say in the mirror before you say it can help because talking to people about medication can lead to anxious feelings. You may have to dig deep and find the energy to tell people it is your choice, and you do not want to discuss it anymore. While you are going through the grieving process, you must take care of your own needs first, even if that is something you have never done before.

"My best friend, who was there for me before my twin died, no longer talks to me or avoids me. Why can't my friend support me?"

When my best friend lost a twin, I felt helpless and clueless. I was afraid to think I could relate but also wanted to let her know I was thinking of her. At times, I avoided asking because I wondered if I asked how she was doing, she might feel obligated to talk to me. I am a therapist and struggled to know what to do. I say that because I want you to know that just because others may avoid you, it does not mean they do not love you. Sometimes, we must teach people what we need. And when you are grieving, you are already extended beyond your abilities. So, sometimes, in the process of grief, we must know that friendships can heal and it is imperative that you take care of yourself first.

In the deep, complicated grief of losing a twin, others cannot understand the special nature of twin loss. You may reach out for support from others who have previously been helpful and find that your attempts at receiving support leave you feeling misunderstood and alone. When others have lost a non-twin, they think they can relate to your pain.

The problem is, nothing compares to the loss of a twin. Research indicates that the two worst losses are the death of a spouse and a twin, and most individuals are unable to conceptualize your deep grief.

Some people also think there is a set time for grief. Everyone grieves differently, and others can pressure you into thinking that your time for grief is over. When people feel misunderstood and are in deep grief, they often push people away and isolate themselves. This is normal, but also pushes people away. When you lose a part of yourself, such as a twin, people simply cannot understand because twin loss is something that can only be fully understood by someone who has experienced it.

When possible, you may want to reach out to your friend and ask them why they are avoiding you. Your friend may feel hopeless and not know what to do, which is normal for someone who cannot understand what is happening. In your grief and shock, you may have neglected your friend or alluded that they couldn't help you. Some best friends can feel left out when you discuss your twin and they will avoid you because they feel hurt. Others who make your grief about them make your grieving harder. You barely have the strength to shower and do daily tasks, much less explain yourself or try to console someone else. It is all normal, though. People who love you have their own feelings about what you are going through. You are still in a delicate place, though. The key is to meet your own needs first and then try to mend your relationships when you are feeling better.

"I feel all alone. Even in my support group, I feel like no one understands me. Will anyone ever understand me?"

Feeling alone and misunderstood is a normal part of grieving. But, when you are grieving the loss of a twin, grief is complicated, and this makes feeling understood even more difficult. Twin death is not as common as non-twin sibling death. Because twin death is less common than other death and has unique and challenging aspects of the grieving process, it is difficult for others to understand your pain.

Research indicates that monozygotic (identical) twins can have a more difficult grieving process than dizygotic (not identical) twins. If you are an MZ twin, you may struggle to relate even within twin support groups. Some twins feel out of place in their support group if they are trying to relate to individuals who are not experiencing complicated grief. If your support group is for grief and not twin loss, you may continue to feel misunderstood. Losing a twin is different than other loss, and it requires a special understanding. I strongly suggest reaching out to organizations such as Twinless Twins (www.twinlesstwins.org) to assist you in finding a twin loss support group.

There is extreme loneliness after the loss of a twin. Everyone copes with the loss of a twin differently and on a different timeline. It is reasonable to want to feel understood, but sometimes it is better for healing to focus on the attempts at support. Getting wrapped up in feelings of brokenness and loneliness can lead to an extended period of grief and pain. Non-twin relatives and friends can also become impatient with the enduring grief that comes from twin loss, so it is crucial to remember that your situation is unique and to meet your own needs in healthy ways such as joining a twin support group or finding a counselor with experience working with twin loss.

"I don't understand why some people claim to see signs or often dream of their twin and I don't. Why can they experience this and I can't?"

This is a difficult question to answer due to the religious and cultural aspects of different individuals. Some cultures or religions believe in signs from the afterlife, and different individuals have different belief systems regarding dreams. Some individuals believe that if you see a loved one in a dream, that means their loved one has a troubled spirit. Some individuals believe that different animals or events can be a sign that their loved one is protecting them in spirit. I do not want to disrespect individual cultural or religious beliefs so I will discuss this question from the perspective of my experience with working with twin loss.

I have worked with many individuals experiencing grief and trauma. When loss and grief cause mental distress, people often reach out to others to try and make sense of their pain and to try and normalize their pain. As a result, people report feeling different and "messed up" if their experience is not the same as another person's experience. Because everyone's grieving process is different, it is not productive to compare your experience with someone else's. You may process grief and loss in a way that does not include signs and dreams.

Many people who experience the loss of a twin feel the same way as you and do not have signs of their twin or have their twins visit them in their dreams. Our minds attempt to process information in several different ways. Some researchers believe that dreaming is our brain's attempt to process information. However, many people do not dream nor can they remember their dreams. Many twins do not see signs of their deceased twin. It is important to evaluate why this is important to you and try to fill that need differently. Some people are hoping for a sign that their twin is still with them in spirit. Some are trying to make sure their twin is not forgotten. Some alternative exercises are to journal about your memories with your twin, put together a scrapbook, or talk to other loved ones about memories with your twin.

"My family thinks it is crazy to mourn a twin I never met. My twin died at birth, and I am 40 years old."

Your family's reaction is a common reaction for people who are unaware of the deep connection that forms in the womb. The twin bond begins at conception. Many twins discuss a sense that they are emotionally connected to a twin they never met or do not remember meeting. Not only do they share genes, but they also shared a womb and began developing together before they were conscious of knowing each other. Some twins feel a sense of sadness or emotional pain from a very early age and then later find out they lost a twin sibling at birth or shortly after. Many early-loss twins feel a sense that a part of them is missing long before they learn they had a twin who died. What you are feeling is normal, and it is part of twin loss. The more you deny the validity of your pain, the longer it can last.

The first step in healing womb twin loss is to recognize that your pain is valid and to allow yourself to grieve. Make sure that you do not feel that you are to blame for your twin's loss. Some families tell a twin that they took all their sibling's nutrition. In grief, some parents or siblings can act as if it is your fault your twin died, even to the point of victimizing you through emotional abuse. Some parents and family members are unable to deal with the pain of loss, so they just ignore it, and they want you to "get over it" or "stop talking about it." It may be that your family is having a difficult time processing the pain, so they are avoiding it. It may be that they are unable to understand because they did not develop with another person as you did. Whatever the reason, you must forgive yourself for surviving and allow yourself to grieve your twin. Some people find that planning and having a funeral is helpful. You can also reach out to others in groups such as Twinless Twins so that you can find support and understanding for the pain you are feeling. Your family may not be able to assist you in the way you need help, so it is important to seek help outside of your family.

"Someone I know lost a twin, and I do not know what to do. I feel like I can't help. What can I do?"

First, do not judge their pain. Even if you are the parent of the twins, your pain and grieving may be different than that of an individual who lost their twin. One of the most common things twins discuss needing after the loss of a twin is someone to listen and the space to grieve in their own way. Because no two people grieve in the same way, you can often help individuals by meeting them where they are and not telling them what you think they should do.

Because twin loss can sometimes feel unexplainable, just giving someone your full attention and listening without feedback is often what helps the most. Ask your friend or family member what they need and try to take any associated pressures off them, such as making sure they don't have to comfort you in your pain and loss. Try to cook and clean (if the person has trouble with daily tasks) and try to help with children if necessary. When you reach out to check on them, please just say things such as, "I am thinking of you, no need for a response." That way, if the person is having a bad day or struggling, they don't have to use their energy trying to make others feel better or answer calls or messages.

Be prepared for odd behaviors and a lot of intense, changing emotions. Please do not take things personally and try to understand that when a person loses a twin, they lose a part of themselves. Imagine what it must feel like for them, but also know that unless you've experienced the loss of a twin, you cannot fully grasp their pain. You can, however, listen to them and understand that what they are saying is their truth. Remember that mostly, they need to feel heard and understood. If you notice any behaviors such as extreme isolation, lack of appetite, sleeping a lot or not sleeping, lack of self-care (bathing, etc.), and extreme uncontrollable emotion, please consider the possibility that your loved one may need some professional help. Some people offer transportation or financial assistance so that the person can get the help they need.

Some of the biggest complaints from twins who have lost twins are that their family does not understand them, tells them they should be done grieving, or tries to tell them what to do without listening to what they are feeling. Others who have experienced twin loss or have knowledge of and experience in twin loss may be able to help them the most. Allow them to grieve on their timeline, not yours. Try to help them discuss memories of their twin, but also respect that they need to stop talking about them sometimes so that they can manage their grief.

Look for signs of suicidal thoughts, such as talking about how people would be better off without them or giving their or their twin's possessions away. If you suspect someone is planning or has attempted suicide, please call 911 or take them to the nearest emergency room. Do not try to make them feel bad or guilty for those thoughts, and do not try to stop them on your own. Call for help and take the person seriously if they discuss suicide or start showing signs of suicidal thoughts or intent. The American Foundation for Suicide Prevention has a list of signs and symptoms, along with resources for what to do (https://afsp.org/about-suicide/risk-factors-and-warning-signs/). The National Suicide Prevention Hotline is 1-800-273-8255 and is available 24 hours a day.

I Might Not See You, But I Can Feel You

For thirty-two years my best friend, Shannon Miller, held a secret. I have known her for twenty of those years and thought I knew everything there was to know about her. Shannon had twin baby girls in 1986. Lacie Lenece, the tiniest of the two, died at birth due to Twin-to-Twin Transfusion Syndrome. Shannon was very young and, at the time, didn't have enough money for a standard wooden casket for Lacie's burial. Therefore, she was provided with a Styrofoam casket in its place. A tiny metal cross was taped to the outside of the box, as a symbol of faith and eternal existence of God being present in this innocent infant's soul. As Shannon told me this story many times before, she would always cry when she remembered how the casket wiggled and squeaked as they carried baby Lacie to the grave site. It was a memory so traumatizing for the young mom that she said she would never forget it. After the service, Shannon secretly took the little cross from the top and put it in her purse. She carried the metal cross in her purse for thirty-two years. This token of Lacie's eternal life lived within Shannon's soul, it is in the stories that wake her up at night, and is part of the story that wove together what makes her who she is today.

When she shared this story of the cross with me, I couldn't believe she never mentioned it before. I knew about Lacie and how Shannon suffered as a young mother but never knew about this special token. I mean, come on, we are best friends, how could she not tell me something so beautiful? After Neva passed, I struggled through anger, vulnerability, sadness, and weakness. I now understand why it was so difficult for Shannon to share her most intimate story with other people. I too carry a secret, and I want to share it with you.

In this collection, I am proud to have shared mine and Neva's life together and my struggles after her death. Some of the feelings I expressed may sound crazy or unbelievable, like when I mentioned spirits and paranormal presence around me. As absurd as these scenarios sound, they were and are very real to me. I hope that by explaining this gift, you may understand why you too see or believe in "signs." If nothing else, I hope you read my words without judgment and know that we all cope and manage grief in our own ways. You may have something you are ashamed of admitting, and I am here to tell you not to let fear of judgment hold you from experiencing your twin. I know that I will no longer let my fear of judgment keep me from experiencing my Neva.

According to my beliefs and research on the topic, a loved one who recently dies will be anxious to let us know they are okay and are aware of what's happening in our lives. If we cannot sense their presence, they'll often give us a "sign" that we can't ignore. These signs lead us to believe there is a message from our loved one. Even if we dismiss it, that little voice inside will make us wonder about the intent.

The gift of being able to sense these signs and presence around me grew stronger once Neva died. I had never given much thought to it other than the awareness that I could sense when a spirit was nearby. After Neva's death, however, I feverishly researched what was I experiencing and learned I held three gifts: Clairvoyance, Clairsentience, and Clairaudience.

Clairvoyance is psychic messages received via pictures, images, or colors. It is not something you see with your naked eye but rather this "third eye." My clairvoyance has always been described as the fact that I can see the person or image in detail, in my mind. I don't physically see it, but I imaginatively see it. The few nights before Neva passed I realized her room was full of spirits. I could see shapes and could identify their ages but did not recognize any of them. A young boy stood out the strongest. He appeared to be about twelve years old. To this day I am puzzled by who he was and why he stood out from the rest. In another experience, I was presented with an image of my husband's friend. I didn't talk to the man often, but I knew he didn't look well in the image. I urged my husband to reach out, only to find out the man had suffered from a massive stroke.

When I lived in Ohio with Neva, my husband and I were restoring an old house. My husband was the biggest skeptic of spirits or anything supernatural, so I never discussed much of my beliefs with him, until this point in our lives. Things started happening in our old home that could not be explained. He began to witness them after I told him what I had felt and sensed. There was an elderly man, very tall, and I would see him in a very specific part of the house. Remember, I didn't physically see him, I saw him with my mind. Neva was very talented in construction and would often assist in our restoration project. During one visit, she was working in the bathroom of the house when I received her phone call. She said "Eva, I am leaving and never going in that house alone again." Of course, I asked her what happened. She went on to tell me that a man was in the house with her. She described him and pinpointed the location where she saw him. She described him in the exact way I had described to my husband. Our experiences with this man made a believer out of my husband. This was a very physical spirit that no one could ignore.

I finally gained the courage to ask the former home owners if anyone had passed away in the house or if they had any experiences like ours. The man who formerly lived there immediately reached out confirming that, although he didn't experience anything, his sister-in-law was "gifted" and never went back to the house after initially visiting.

Clairsentience is the sense of "knowing" and it is very familiar to most people. It is like walking into a room where an argument just took place and the room gets deadly quiet. You know something just happened there, right? Of course, you can feel the tension or emotion. What happens in this situation is you are feeling the thoughts and actions of others' auras. As I did for many years as a young adult, one day I was walking on my college campus that was filled with other students. As you can imagine, on a college campus it's not unusual to bump into someone you know quite frequently. This particular day I was walking to the food court and my arm touched another student. He was male and his eyes met mine as we accidently bumped each other. As our eyes met, however, I experienced an instant sense of evil. His aura exuded pure evil. Two days later I received a notice from the university about a rape reported on campus. The photograph of the man was the same man I had bumped in to only days before. Call it coincidence if you will, but I have only felt pure evil a few times in my life and that instance shook me to the core. Clairsentience is often compared to instinct or intuition. You read a situation, develop a conclusion, but decide to ignore it because it doesn't seem realistic. You may also experience clairsentience if you've ever been driving and you suddenly decide to take an alternate route for whatever reason, and then later find out there was a fatal accident on your usual route. Instinct?

Clairaudience is usually heard internally (in your head.) Sometimes, clairaudient messages can be heard with your "regular hearing." But remember, the dead no longer have a physical body, therefore, they don't need a physical voice. Have you heard someone calling your name? Most people would disregard that. I listen! I want to know what it is my spirits are trying to tell me. My messages are always heard in my own voice.

I have always struggled with a super busy mind. I can spend a day driving with no music just looking at my surroundings and talking to myself. I see old buildings and think about what they could become new again, great business ideas in certain locations. I used to believe this was a talent or niche I must have had for business and marketing. It turns out I have a strong sense of clairaudience. I love music and enjoy writing my own work. It makes me feel connected to my soul. I learn best through the auditory channel. I prefer listening rather than reading. Too much noise makes me feel drained or irritable. Do you ever hear ringing in your ears or a high-pitched sound, yet there is no medical reason? (This might be your spirit guides trying to get your attention.)

My Son, Noah, was four years old when he began telling me about his friend "Jonathan." Noah would rush home from preschool to tell me all about his adventurous day with Jonathan; this carried on for months. Once day, Noah and Jonathan got in a fight, which devastated Noah. He was distraught that Jonathan wouldn't play with him anymore. I decided to talk with his preschool teacher about it to see how we could resolve the disagreement. I started explaining my concerns to Ms. Pat, Noah's teacher. She immediately looked perplexed and explained that there was no student named Jonathan. She, also, had been hearing stories about the mystery child but believed he was a neighborhood friend. I decided to gently talk to Noah about Jonathan asking him who he was. My four-year-old, I remind you, proceeded to tell me that Jonathan moved here from California after he was terribly shot. How could a rambunctious, innocent child carry on, day after day, for months, talking about a child that didn't exist?

It is common today to hear that children have imaginary friends. The details of these friendships are very much believed by the children, as if they are in a different realm. Noah is twenty-one now and he openly speaks about his experience with Jonathan. It is obvious that he carries this special gift like me.

Why do some have the gift and some don't?

Science suggests that the right side of the brain is the "intuitive side." As we grow and are influenced by family, teachers, peers, and society, we use our intuitive side less and less. The left side of the brain, the "analytical side," becomes stronger because of our fading intuition. It is believed that everyone starts out with a psychic gift; the gift evolves, declines, or changes as we absorb information in our own way. Some people become skeptical of these gifts and end up not believing at all. However, it is more common that people continue to believe, develop, or question their gift throughout their lifetime. If you believe that you have been given a gift, I recommend seeking a support group of those who carry similar beliefs. There is no reason to feel judged or "crazy." If you're like me, then you know that these gifts keep you connected to your twin. Living in judgment or constantly feeling like you are being evaluated is not healthy. Surrounding yourself with like-minded people you can share your gift with will help you tremendously.

What if you can't see these signs or sense their presence around you?

People often overlook signs for various reasons, a lot of times it's out of their control. A few of these reasons include:

(1) the attempts for contact aren't always what people expect them to be; (2) people are scared and don't believe in the unknown or unseen; or (3) as in a lot of cases, people's logical mind finds a sensible explanation for the sign, even when the explanation may not make much sense either. It's easier for us to rationalize the action, rather than accept it for what it may truly be. Are you an analytical person? If so, you may have the toughest time receiving messages because your brain rationalizes and analyzes the attempt to be something more plausible. My advice for you is to try living your life with an open mind, watch for signs and communication, continue sending your twin love, and, above all else, don't be discouraged if you fail to dream about them or receive messages right away. These things take time and patience. Just have an open mind and heart and allow presence into your soul.

My sister-in-law, Brenda, badly desired these gifts and wished to see a sign from Neva, but she was skeptical and never believed in "those things" before. Like many others, she was confused by the thought of spiritual presence after death, but she was in pain and deeply longed for a connection to Neva. I could hear the pain and jealously in her voice when I would talk about my visits with Neva. She was struggling from losing her wife and would give anything to feel or see her for a brief second. After talking to Brenda many times about allowing belief in her heart, I recommended that she see a reputable medium for support. Honestly, I never believed in the work of mediums before but, with my heightened spiritual awareness and joy that I found by seeing Neva after she died, I figured there was no harm in suggesting this to Brenda. So, she made the appointment to see a very well-known and respected medium in Ohio. The woman's professional credentials were astonishing and appointments were booked three months in advance. Brenda was saddened during her first visit because Neva did not come through right away. However, amazingly, Neva found Brenda through the medium on the second attempt. Brenda cried as the medium validated Neva's appearance by drawing the person she was communicating with. Right in front of Brenda's eyes, the medium quickly sketched a woman who longed to find Brenda. This validation is very rare and unusual in the profession. The only thing this lady knew was that she was doing a reading with Brenda. No last names or photographs were given at any time prior to the reading. By allowing herself to experience this validation, Brenda is now more open to signs around her and has even shared some of her feelings of Neva's presence. This would have never happened had she not opened her mind and heart to being more sensitive and receptive.

I know now firsthand what it is like to lose someone you deeply love. Likewise, I know even more so what it's like to feel like you're never going to see or talk to them again. But nothing could be further from the truth. The dead don't leave us, they just change form. Do your best to open your heart to receive their signs and allow yourself to receive their communication. Always send your love when you find yourself thinking you experienced a sign. Who knows . . . you may feel some love coming down to you too.

If you have a gift and experience positive signs and presence, don't let another's judgment and disbelief destroy what you have left with your loved one.

Moving Forward

I somehow have an innate ability to compartmentalize. I put my head down and dig in to the task at hand. This is something I have done in pretty much every aspect and event in my life. When I set my mind to a task nothing else matters until the task is complete. I couldn't help but question myself while working on this book. Was this compartmentalization just masking my grief? When the book is done will I return to that dark place that started my writing in the first place?

The answer is no. Writing has allowed me to express my feelings and communicate with Neva, albeit a one-way conversation. I use a journal and write in free form style. Sometimes I am writing to Neva and sometimes I am expressing anger, shock, dismay, regret – all the emotions one feels after the death of a loved one.

I started writing out of a strong personal need to help others with their grief. In return, I have found a way to help with my own grief long term. I hope to never quit creating as creating through our grief will help us to survive.

The sad days that surround us will become fewer and fewer as time goes by and they will be filled with new memories. As I take my nightly walks alone, well almost alone, I talk to Neva and reminisce about things we did growing up. She seems to always bring about a memory of something I had forgotten. I smile and cry as I am walking with her memory. Every walk, every day gets better and better and then a bad day comes along. We will never be able to escape them because our love for our twins is so deep.

My friendships with other twins has undeniably been my life saver. So, I would like to end with things I have learned from other twins.

Things I learned about loss from other twins

* I am not alone. I have found emotional and physical support in a safe and non-judgmental environment.

* Twins provide support and understanding from others who have experienced a similar loss.

* I can begin the healing process through sharing my own story and hearing the stories of other twins.

* I found hope through companionship with people who "get it" and understand first-hand what I'm going through.

* There is opportunity to discover new traditions and ideas to keep my twin present in my heart and in my memories.

* I have an increased understanding of how children and other family members react to loss.

* I have permission to grieve and permission to live a happy productive life.
* Your pain is "real" and not just in your head. This loss is a true broken heart and, in time, the pain lessens yet never gone. – Sue Rice
* Twins are used to sharing everything and are incredibly unselfish.

May God protect and watch over us all in our journey of healing. - Eva Sombathy

Self Help

I find that sharing and reflecting on Neva and my life together has positively affected my healing in the grief process. On my worst days, when I am hopeless and the pain is unbearable, I use reflection exercises to pull me out of the darkness. Here are a few helpful activities to support you through your darkest days. Keep them handy – they become fun memories to read over and over again!

Memorial Stones

Write down important dates that have shaped you and your twin's lives (marriages, births of each other's children, baptisms, etc.). Reflecting on special dates are a great reminder of precious and positive events that you have shared.

_____

_____

_____

_____

_____

_____

_____

_____

_____

_____

_____

_____

_____

_____

_____

_____

_____

_____

_____

_____

_____

_____

_____

_____

Memories

Write down some of the funniest things you remember about your twin. I try reflecting on each age and the phases of our lives. What happened in elementary school? Middle school? High school? College? Your special dates from the former exercise may also bring out some funny ones…

_____

_____

_____

_____

_____

_____

_____

_____

_____

_____

_____

_____

_____

_____

_____

_____

_____

_____

_____

_____

_____

_____

_____

_____

Resources

National Suicide Prevention Hotline (USA) – available 24/7/365 1-800-273-8255 www.suicidepreventionlifeline.org

Befrienders Worldwide - Suicide Prevention Across the Globe Provides access to support online and by phone in all countries. www.befrienders.org

Twinless Twins Support Group International™ (TTSGI) www.twinlesstwins.org

Lone Twin Network

www.lonetwinnetwork.org.uk

Rewrite You Story Counseling

Carolyn J Burleson, MA, MS, LPC, LCDC, MA

1-830-357-8933

www.rewriteyourstorycounseling.com

Barbara Klein, Ph.D.

Gifted Children & Twins | School Placement & Parent Coaching | Educational Consultant Since 1986 | Los Angeles, CA

www.drbarbaraklein.squarespace.com/

Books:

Living Without Your Twin by Betty Jean Case

The Lone Twin: Understanding Twin Bereavement and Loss by Joan Woodward

The Psychic Navigator: Harnessing Your Inner Guidance by John Holland

Alone in the Mirror: Twins in Therapy by Dr. Barbara Klein

Extras

A few fun memories that personify twin life and twin fun submitted by twinless twin friends.

Marylon and Carylon

Michael and Michelle

Darlene, Twin to David 1961-2008

Mallory and Sean

HOLIDAYS

The ton-up twins'! My beloved twin Lyn is on the bike. I'm (Jean) in the side car.

ROAD TRIP!
KACY AND KAYLA

Tresa and Tracy
`MERICA`

Karen and Lisa

Deb and Di

Susan and Kathy

KIT, BETH AND ERIN

Wilmette and Wilma

Sweethearts

Chance and Chelsea

"Born together,
Best friends forever."

Martin &Helene

Charla
&
Carla

Jill and Julie

CHRISTY & MISTY

RONALD
AND
DONALD

Jennifer's remberance

Katy's Keepsake

Shannon's Angel.....
Crystal's Sister

Madison and Maya

Jennifer & Melissa

Susan

Carol

Lisa and Teresa

Sandra & Barbara

Adrienne and Andrea

Susan
& Beth

Bonnie and Connie

Jim and Gayle

Shawn and Barbie

Raymond & Rene

Till We Meet Again

Judy and Julie

Susan and Michael

ETHAN
EMILY

Stacie and Stephanie

RACHEAL AND RYAN

RONNEY & ROLLY

Amy & Amber

Luci and Luke

Eli & Ellie

Kim & Michelle

Diane, twin to Denise

Dina & Tina

Cathy & Linda

" Nothing better than Being together"

Angel and Michelle

Melissa and Sheri Lynn

Rebeca and Beatriz

Sandy & Candy

LAURA & LINDA

Karen and Lisa

TAMMY & TARA

JESSICA & BRITTANY

Barbie and Shawn

TASHA AND TONYA

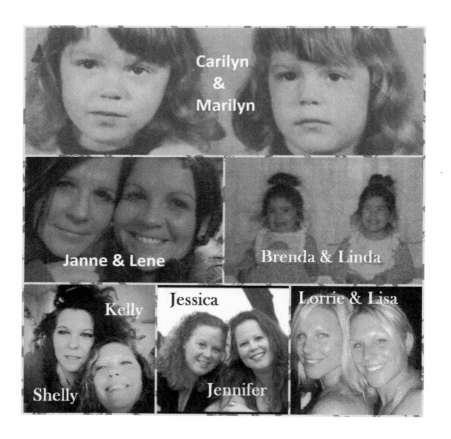

Hal and Jan

Patty and Mike

Maggie and Colin

Pana and Irine

Don and Linda

Rebecca, twin to Robert

Amanda & Ashley

Pamela & Pat

Melanie & Andrea

Jackie and Jennifer

SUNDAY AND CINDY

SHEILA AND SHEENA

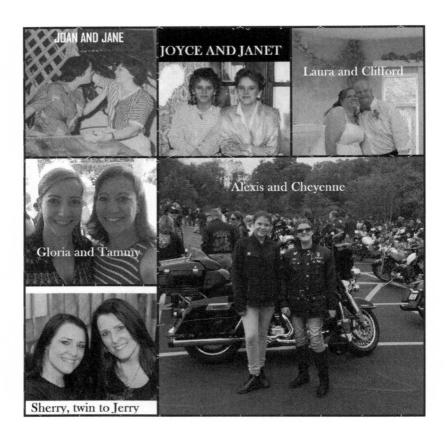

JOAN AND JANE

JOYCE AND JANET

Laura and Clifford

Gloria and Tammy

Alexis and Cheyenne

Sherry, twin to Jerry

Savannah & Lucas

Karin and Erik

Lisa and Dustin

Erik and Erin

Laurie and Frankie

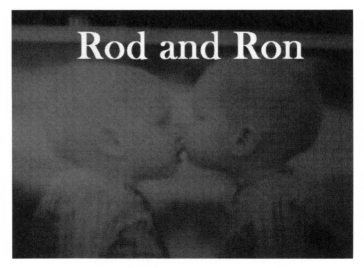

Rod and Ron

Neva and Brenda in Florida

Neva on her last trip to Florida

Letter to My Neva on our birthday

Dear Neva,

Happy Birthday. Here we are at 50!! Time seems to just keep on flying by. I am saddened that I must celebrate such a big milestone without you, and I can't help but cry as I sit here thinking about the past 15 months without you by my side. It has been difficult to say the least, I mean really difficult. On days like today, where the pain is unbearable, I try to remind myself of the great memories we have shared. We really had a fun life together, didn't we?

Remember when we lived on Sweetbriar? We would make torches or grab flashlights to explore the storm tunnels around town. We spent countless hours in those tunnels, pretending the city was going to open a mysterious flood gate, trapping us down there forever.

Remember all the go-karts and forts we built from wood we had collected from nearby construction sites? I had my first kiss from a neighborhood boy in one of those forts, and then you ran home to tell Dad. Tattle Tale!

What about our one-and-only fight we got into in middle school? We both got suspended for 3 days. Ha!

Remember 8th grade graduation? There just happened to be a food fight in the cafeteria beforehand, and I just happened to get caught in the middle of it. The Principal wouldn't let me walk across the stage at graduation and I was devastated! Do you remember Mom making me wear our matching graduation outfit even though I had to sit out? HA! I cried so hard watching you walk across that stage. Of course, history repeated itself when I watched you walk across the stage at high school graduation. My karma, I suppose, for leaving you that final year.

Remember our first job when we were 15? Burger King. We lied about our age so we could work and make money. We made a great team, didn't we? "Mayo, lettuce, tomato – pickle, ketchup, onion" – I'll never forget. Mom and Dad thought we were always working the late-shift but we would really be out with friends.

Remember the time eight of us squeezed into Dede's VW and drove to Oklahoma, just because we could? Geez, that was incredibly dangerous.

Remember your first boyfriend? He had that stinky Ford Bronco. I always ended up sitting in the back smelling the leaky exhaust. Yuck!

Remember holding April for the first time? Boy did you think she was yours... and you took her on her first Halloween because I had to work. I thank you had more fun than she did. We were so young!

Remember when you left for the Army? You didn't want to get all emotional about it. '*See ya later, Butthead!*' is what you said as you left. That was our first big separation.

129

Remember your wedding day? Randy had never ridden a horse before then, but you insisted on getting married on horseback. I will never forget the fear in that man's eyes - hahahaha!

I could go on and on with the memories but I will save them for our next birthday. OK, actually, here's one more.

Remember how we planned our retirement years ago? Florida - on a beach! We imagined you dragging an oxygen tank down the beach because you had smoked too much, and then me carrying my dumbbells while sweating to oldies music. Well sister, guess what? This year I moved to Florida! I feel you with me as I walk down the beach and think about how much you would love it here. It frequently saddens me knowing that this chapter of my life will only be as a half... where is my twinsie to walk down the beach with me? If only I could have you here one last time...

I miss you more than words can describe. Just promise to wait on me up there! I can't wait until we get to experience another lifetime together!

I miss you, butthead! Cheers to 50!

Love,
Eva

My dream: "Pick your chin up and get busy living"
- Neva Clark

Artwork by Rocco Minichino

References

Barar, D. (2018). My Later Abortion Of One Twin Saved Our Daughter's Life. This Is Our Story. [Blog] *Scary Mommy*. Available at: https://www.scarymommy.com/later-abortion-saved-daughters-life/.

Barnett, D. (2018). *Daryl and Dawn*. Personal communication.

Burleson, C. (2018). Personal communication.

Stark, R. (2017). *for when… a twin sibling dies*. [online] twinloss nz. Available at: https://twinlossnz.wordpress.com/2012/02/29/for-when-a-twin-sibling-dies/.

Cincinnatichildrens.org. (2018). *Twin-Twin Transfusion Syndrome (TTTS) | Cincinnati Fetal Center | Cincinnati Children's Hospital Medical Center*. [online] Available at: https://www.cincinnatichildrens.org/service/f/fetal-care/conditions/twin-twin-transfusion-syndrome [Accessed 18 Jul. 2018].

Cohen, D. (1996). *Lose your twin, live half a life.* [online] The Independent. Available at: https://www.independent.co.uk/news/lose-your-twin-live-half-a-life-1308798.html.

Cowan, R. (2018). *18 years ago today I saw you last..* [online] Facebook.com. Available at: https://www.facebook.com/notes/rod-cowan/18-years-ago-today-i-saw-you-last/10153374989134064/.

CDC.gov. (2017). *FastStats - Multiple Births.* [online] Available at: https://www.cdc.gov/nchs/fastats/multiple.htm [Accessed 18 Jul. 2018].

Fitzwater, C. H. (2018). *Charla and Carla.* Personal communication.

Hewell, C. (2018). *Crystal and Lacie.* Personal communication.

Piontelli, A. (1989). A study of twins before and after birth. *The International review of Psycho-Analysis*, 16, pp.413-426. https://www.independent.co.uk/news/lose-your-twin-live-half-a-life-1308798.html ;

Roemelt, A. (2011). You can't miss what you never had. [Blog] *Enjy's Place.* Available at: http://enjysplace.blogspot.com/2011/04/you-cant-miss-what-you-never-had.html?m=0.

Twinlesstwins.org. *Twinless Twins Support Group International.* [online] Available at: http://www.twinlesstwins.org.

Why Grieving Has No Time Limit

Aug 10, 2017 | Funeral Insights, Support Grief has no time limit: https://www.deadright.com/grieving-no-time-limit/.

Contact Information

Eva Jo Sombathy

evajo@amewithoutwe.com

www.amewithoutwe.com

www.facebook.com/amewithoutwe

Made in the USA
Middletown, DE
12 March 2020